Exposed

Confessions of a Wedding Photographer

Exposed

Confessions of a Wedding Photographer

A MEMOIR

Claire Lewis

THOMAS DUNNE BOOKS ✿ NEW YORK
ST. MARTIN'S PRESS

In some cases people's names and physical characteristics have been changed or composited to preserve the individual's privacy. Certain events have been altered, compressed, or presented out of sequence, to avoid causing embarrassment or hurt. None of the photographs that appear in the book are of the people whose stories I tell.

THOMAS DUNNE BOOKS.
An imprint of St. Martin's Press.

www.thomasdunnebooks.com
www.stmartins.com

Photo on page 33 courtesy of Jill T. Johnson. Photo on page 61 courtesy of Stuart Kogod. Photo on page 199 courtesy of Beatrice Landolt.

Book design by Spring Hoteling

Library of Congress Cataloging-in-Publication Data

Lewis, Claire, photographer.
    Exposed : confessions of a wedding photographer / Claire Lewis.—1st ed.
        p. cm.
    ISBN-13: 978-0-312-38189-9
    ISBN-10: 0-312-38189-1
    1. Wedding photography.   I. Title.

TR819 .L47 2008
770.92—dc22

                                        2008007508

First Edition: June 2008

10 9 8 7 6 5 4 3 2 1

For my mother,
Ewa Lewis

Contents

Contents

Acknowledgments

First and foremost, my thanks to the couples who trusted me to document their wedding day and provided me with so many interesting hours and such a wealth of material. Particular thanks are due to the couples who allowed me to use their wedding photographs in the book, and to Scott and Haley, who generously agreed to model for me. Because readers may naturally wonder—no, none of the people pictured are related to those whose stories I tell here.

It is my great good fortune that my agent is Andrea Somberg. I don't know how I got so lucky as to have such an astute, witty, and absolutely terrific person on my side, but I'm awfully glad I do.

I am grateful as well that my editor is Toni Plummer. *Exposed* has improved every step of the way due to her skill, sharp eye, and hard work.

Acknowledgments

Bonnie Chernin, beautiful writer and kind friend, gave me encouragement and good advice with great generosity of spirit.

Anthony Bruno and Judith Sachs kindly offered me the benefit of their friendship and experience.

For many years now Karen McLean has been both a friend and an inspiration. She reminds me by her example that passion's the thing.

Tia Gavin was there for almost everything that happens in *Exposed,* and could tell a few stories of her own! She is a dear and treasured friend. I'm grateful to her for many acts of kindness, much wise counsel, and various bits of inspired artistic collaboration, and for making my life considerably more fun. She's family.

I owe a particular debt of gratitude to Carolyn Lewis and Robert Acosta-Lewis for the many times they have propped me up, sorted me out, taken me in, and told me they loved me no matter what. Just the way I love them.

Finally, I want to thank John and Tess. They both know exactly how I feel about them, so I won't go into it here. Suffice it to say that my life with the two of them is a wonderment of riches, and their patience and good humor while I was writing this book were positively heroic. Sweet is the melody, my best beloveds.

Exposed

Confessions of a Wedding Photographer

Introduction

The Wedding Photographer

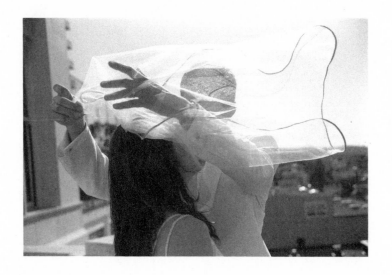

The elevator glides upward smoothly. Moments later, the doors slide open on the eighteenth floor of a San Francisco high-rise hotel. Stepping out, I swing my camera bag over my shoulder and walk to the door of the Golden Gate Suite. Here I stop and take a deep breath. I know what's behind that door.

The air is thick with hair spray and Victoria's Secret perfume. It's an asthmatic's nightmare. "Mom, my inhaler," gasps a voice. That must be the bride. She's wearing shorts, a huge updo, and pearls. Nothing else. She sucks deeply on her inhaler as the stylist sends a cloud of hair spray drifting down over them both. Ten women in matching lemon yellow sweat suits with BRIDESMAID embroidered across the backside are in various states of undress, panic, and bad temper. "I need a Valium," moans a sweating bridesmaid with a Lycra girdle halfway up to its final destination. A bridesmaid so thin she's practically transparent looks at her without sympathy. "Valium you can buy. Exactly how am I supposed to get boobs in the next fifteen minutes?" The coordinator rushes over with double-stick tape and a pair of breast pads. "No problem, honey, we'll just stick these right on. That'll keep your dress up. And don't you worry," she says soothingly to the chubby bridesmaid who has finally managed to get the girdle up over her bottom. "I've got some Valium right here." From the bathroom someone yells, "Hey, can I get some help here, please? I need makeup on my back to cover these zits!"

Everyone's jewelry is either missing, broken, or just plain wrong. No one can agree on how the sashes on the dresses should be tied. The flowers are late. In one corner, a panty-hose versus no-panty-hose argument is raging. The bride's makeup needs an extra half hour to complete, and the coordinator has forgotten the brand of bottled water the bride expressly asked for. The ring bearer is happily killing people with a noisy video game, and the flower girl is crying because someone just stabbed her with a bobby pin while attaching her head wreath. The bride's mother dashes up and grabs my arm. "Are you the photographer?" I freeze. Am I? Yup, that's me.

$\mathcal{I}$ am a wedding photographer. There it is, in black and white. It's not that I mind being a wedding photographer. It's just that if I see it there on the page, I have to admit everything that I'm not. Not a crusading photojournalist. Not a portraitist to the stars. Not on assignment for *National Geographic,* or traveling to distant places to document the miseries of the world's unfortunates. I shoot weddings, and on almost any weekend I can be found in the high-stress world of heightened emotions, familial tension, exaggerated ex-

4

pectations, and mood-softening medications, which surround this ancient and fraught ritual. It's not exactly the sort of cutting-edge photography I once imagined myself doing, but it certainly does have an edge all its own.

My world is populated by brides having anxiety attacks, mothers who try to exorcise the memory of their own botched ceremonies by creating perfect ones for their daughters, and grooms who give themselves stab wounds while trying to pin on their own boutonnieres. I document groomsmen who seduce brides, bridesmaids who seduce groomsmen, brides who change their mind or pass out or dance on tables wearing tiaras. I've seen a fat bulldog faint while wearing a skintight tuxedo and a flower girl bitten by a rattlesnake. And it makes me wonder, why do we work so hard to spoil our own fun as we let the trappings replace the meaning of the event? Why do we need to marry so publicly, lavishly, and expensively? As a country, America spends about seventy billion dollars a year on weddings. Wedding magazines flourish. The market for wedding cakes and boutonnieres never runs dry.

The fantasies, indeed, are formidable. Couples plan their weddings for a year or more, obsessing about the minutest of details. The color of a tablecloth or tie can cause sleepless nights. Those short on cash go into debt and forgo their honeymoon to try to make the reality of their wedding match the fantasy. Brides see themselves as the stars of their own wedding video, and their ceremony as a chance to be famous, however briefly. Weddings are an *InStyle* magazine layout, a fashion shoot, a music video, a perfect moment in time—anything but the obvious: a glaring setup for over-scheduled disaster.

But I would have quit long ago if that were the whole story. I also work with the funny, excited, irreverent couples who are trying to keep some sense of proportion amid the madness of the world of wedding commerce, people who want a minimum of hassle and a maximum of fun. They soon discover that the business of weddings is not set up for them. There's just not enough profit in simplicity. Far better for business to encourage the exaggeration of expectations, entitlement, and just plain old showing off that pervades the industry. There's money to be made.

It is the tension between expectation and reality that keeps the work interesting. It is also what occasionally—when I come home very late from a particularly horrible event—makes me want to bury my head under my pillow and wake up in a world where weddings no longer exist. But by the next weekend I'm out there again. The truth is I like what I do. And maybe twenty years from now my clients will look at the photographs I took and remember how they felt, not just what things looked like. They might even know by then that the feelings were what mattered. Or maybe they will see that where it all went wrong later was foreshadowed in those moments caught on film, when no one was trying to keep up appearances. I'm not a glamour photographer. I'm not a fashion photographer. I am a storyteller, and the story I tell is the one I see.

1

Tuscania

$\mathcal{K}$ristie came to our first meeting wearing a cloud of gardenia scent and a purple tank top, with BORN TO SHOP written in jewels across her chest. I thought she was holding a baby in her arms, but it turned out that she was cradling a twenty-pocket accordion folder. There were sections labeled "Table Linen Swatches," "Bridesmaids' Shoes," "Cute Table Favors," "Martha Stewart's Secrets," and "Stress-Free Honeymoon Sex." Kristie pulled out a thick stack of magazine clippings from the "Special Photographs I Love" slot. I took a look. There were lots of very tall, very beautiful women.

"These are pictures you like?" I guessed.

"Oh, yes." Kristie looked me straight in the eye and continued with great seriousness. "I love them. This is exactly how I want my wedding pictures to look. I knew the minute I saw your Web site that you could create that for me. But the most important thing you should know about my pictures is that they have to be real. I hate phony stuff."

There were lots of things that Kristie wanted me to know about her.

"I love weddings because they are so emotional and intense. I know you must understand how I feel. I love planning weddings. That's why I've made a huge career decision. When this is all over, I'm going to become a wedding planner myself. My whole life has changed since I started planning my wedding. I feel so centered. I go to the gym more, and my eating habits are totally under control. My friends think I'm psychic, you know, because I sensed your honesty just by looking at your photographs. I know I'll be able to sense other people's honesty for my future clients' weddings as well. People would pay a lot for that. I really do love your pictures." She paused and smiled blindingly. She had the whitest teeth I had ever seen.

"Oh, well, thanks," I managed to say before she started again.

"I always think that a woman should support other women, don't you?"

"Well, sure. In general, I do think so," I started to say, but the question had been rhetorical.

"Women, after all, we're, like, about half the population, right? We need to give each other half the support." She stopped short. "We should get down to business, Claire. You're just too easy to chat to! Now, there should be no posed pictures or glamour stuff. That's not what I'm about. I want the sort of natural spontaneous stuff like in magazines. You see what I mean, don't you?" What I saw was a lot of red flags.

"The work in magazines is actually very carefully styled,"

I told her. "Pictures that look like that don't just happen. There's a lot of lighting and makeup involved in those images. I'm more of a documentary photographer. I hardly do conventional portraits at all if I can help it."

"That's perfect," beamed Kristie, "just what I want. I love the stuff that looks like real life. Here, take another look at my samples and you'll see what I mean."

For the next hour I did my best to explain. I made her tea and went through her clippings one by one.

"See that full moon over the beach? It was digitally painted in behind the couple kissing. I don't do that. I would never, ever use Photoshop to color in the bride's bouquet in a black-and-white shot like they did here. I don't retouch, and I would definitely not ask the groomsmen to form a chorus line and do a high kick the way they're doing in that picture there. I'm really just not sure that my style is right for you." I looked over at her, hoping to see some glimmer of understanding. She looked me in the eye and smiled.

"You are everything I'm looking for in a photographer. Can I give you a hug?"

$\mathcal{I}$ agreed to photograph Kristie's wedding. Sometimes I take a job for the money. That happens when the pile of bills gets too high for me to ignore any longer. This was different. Somehow, Kristie had convinced me. I believed her when she told me that with my brilliant eye I would record her day as no other photographer could. One week later, her signed contract arrived in the mail. There was also a schedule for the day that was twelve pages long and another stack of photographs torn from fashion magazines. They were clipped together with a gardenia-scented note. *Can't wait for the big day,* said the note. It was signed with a smiley face.

*W*eddings are big business. Tuscania Winery knows this. It's hardly a winery at all anymore. More like a mall. There's a store stocked with Tuscania merchandise, an on-site wedding planning department, and a permanent wedding reception tent set up on the property. Tuscania has florists, caterers, bakers, and wedding coordinators. It is one-stop shopping for all your nuptial needs. Weddings move through the place at the speed of light, with three or four ceremonies happening every weekend. An army of khaki-clad dictators, cleverly disguised as wedding facilitators, rushes around with headphones and crackling walkie-talkies, trying to keep the various brides from bumping into each other. There are lots of rules at Tuscania. I hate rules.

When things go wrong at Tuscania, it can be a lot of fun. It's like watching the wrath of the marriage gods as they rebel against the idea of weddings as such grimly managed commerce. This was the site Kristie had chosen for her wedding.

I picked up my assistant, Sarah, at 8:00 A.M. in front of the Mission District Victorian where she has her studio apartment. She climbed into the car looking uncharacteristically cheery for such an early hour.

"This is going to be fun," she said.

"At Tuscania?" I felt grumpy. Sometimes just picking Sarah up in the morning makes me grumpy, since she always looks like she's just back from a yoga retreat somewhere, all blond, tanned, and perfectly fit.

"Oh, come on. We'll just follow our twelve pages of highly detailed instructions and try to have a good time." She turned on the radio and started looking for some music. This was definitely odd. Sarah's usual style in the morning is to wear enormous sunglasses and hide behind a cup of coffee until we are fifteen minutes away from the wedding site. Then she asks for her film and schedule for the day, and that's it for small talk.

"What's up?" I asked.

"I just have a feeling about this one," said Sarah. "It's going to be good."

At Tuscania, we were shown to the bride's dressing room by one of the wedding directors.

"Here we go," said Sarah cheerily as I pushed open the door. There, in a room packed with bridesmaids, lavender tulle, hair dryers, and hot rollers, Kristie was having her makeup done. She looked out at me from under enormous false eyelashes.

"How's my makeup?" Her lips were outlined in dark brown, her face was two shades darker than her neck, and her cheeks were very pink. She was wearing a tiara. It was way too late.

"You look great," I said. "No need to do too much more, right?"

"Oh, we're just getting started," said the makeup artist.

An hour later, we began taking stiff, self-conscious pictures in the hundred-degree heat with Kristie, seven bridesmaids, and a lot of other people who wanted to have their pictures taken and whom Kristie had forgotten to mention.

Kristie was working hard. Her makeup was melting down onto the neck of her white gown. Mitch, her groom, was sulking.

"Calm down, baby," Kristie said, giving him a kiss on the cheek while keeping one eye on the camera. "We'll just do a couple more, OK?"

Mitch had had enough of standing in the midday sun wearing a tuxedo and having his picture taken, he was in no mood to be pleasant.

"Not OK, I'm done here."

"Maybe you should take a little break," Kristie crooned, patting his arm. "We'll start on the family pictures without you. Let's do a few cute ones together in the gazebo when you get back."

Mitch gave a grunt that could have meant anything and left with his best man.

"Men," said Kristie. Her bridesmaids nodded in understanding.

"Five bucks says he doesn't come back," whispered Sarah. I wasn't taking that bet. Sarah and I had both seen Mitch's groomsmen gathered in the parking lot with a bottle of Jack Daniel's.

Kristie gave me a bright smile. "Let's get set up in the gazebo," she said. "That way we'll be all ready for pictures when Mitch comes back."

We all trooped off to the gazebo. Half an hour passed. There was no sign of Mitch.

"Shall we do a few of me alone in the vineyard?" Kristie asked. Her smile looked a bit stiff. "Mitch loves the wine country so much. This whole wedding was his idea, you know. He's been in on the planning right from the start. I told all the girls on the Knot about Mitch, and they all think I'm the luckiest bride they know. He's so involved."

We headed for the vineyard. Sarah shot me a dark look. "This is pathetic," she said. Her good mood had evaporated.

Mitch never arrived. Finally even Kristie realized that he wasn't coming, and she and her bridesmaids went back inside to freshen up. Sarah and I decided to go check out the ceremony site, which is what we were doing when we saw an odd-looking woman floating in our direction. As she drew closer, I realized it was just the flowing sea green dress and multiple shawls she was wrapped in that gave the impression she was being pushed along by the breeze rather than walking.

The Oxford American Dictionary says that an officiant is someone who performs a religious service or ceremony and is typically a priest or minister. Not anymore. An officiant now means anyone who has gone online and has made himself or herself an officiant. It takes hardly any time, and anybody at all can do it. Your plumber, your best friend, your dog walker, or your personal trainer—all are fully qualified in ten minutes and a few clicks of the mouse. The officiant for Kristie and Mitch's wedding was a tall, stringy woman wearing long dangling earrings made from seashells and a dreamy expression. She smiled absently at the space somewhere between Sarah and me.

"I am the celebrant," she said. "You can call me Ariel."

I avoided looking at Sarah and said hello. Since the ceremony was due to start in ten minutes, I got down to business.

"Shall we sort out where you'll be standing so we're sure not to block the guests' view and then just quickly go over the order of everyone's entrance?" I asked.

Ariel's eyes widened. She made a tut-tutting noise, as though reprimanding a child, and shook her head sadly.

"We have not worked together before, have we?" she said gently. "You must realize I have a passion for joining people in this, the most sacred and beautiful of unions of the soul, that springs from my own deeply spiritual consciousness. Where people stand or how they enter is supremely unimportant to me."

At this point Sarah tried to slip away. This sort of talk usually sends her off to check if the bar is open. I caught her just in time.

"Sarah, could you go over the ceremony details with Ariel? I'm going to go and make sure Kristie is all set," I said, and ran.

*O*nce the guests were seated and Kristie and Mitch were standing between two enormous marble urns filled with pink roses, Ariel bowed her head for a moment of silence. Raising her head, she rang a tiny brass bell three times and said, "Let the ceremony begin. I open this glorious day by extending my deep love and fellowship to you who are gathered here. I will now read some sweet details from the private letters that I asked the bride and groom to write to each other and share with me so that I could better come to know them." She paused. Kristie and Mitch looked worried.

"Do you think they knew she was going to read sweet

excerpts from their intimate letters to their two hundred guests?" I whispered to Sarah.

She grinned at me. She was beginning to enjoy herself again. "This is great," she said. "I knew it was going to be a good one."

"Our bride," said Ariel, "is a long-distance runner who often travels to participate in triathlons. Mitch cares faithfully for Fleur, their beloved French bulldog, during her long absences." Someone in the crowd laughed and was quickly hushed.

"The proudest day of Mitch's life," continued Ariel, "was the moment when he proposed to Kristie at the summit of Mount Kilimanjaro and she accepted his pledge of eternal love. This remarkable and public-spirited couple hopes someday to design a vegan running shoe that is not only comfortable but will be affordable to people from every walk of life." Ariel beamed.

"What? What is she saying?" the bride's grandmother asked loudly.

"She said Kristie likes running," the bride's mother shouted into the grandmother's hearing aid.

"Running where?" the grandmother shouted back.

There was more laughter now. Mitch stepped close to Ariel and began to speak to her in a whisper too low for Ariel's body mike to pick up.

"What's he saying? I gotta know what he's saying," said Sarah. Not being able to hear was making her nuts.

Sarah and I focused our zoom lenses in on Ariel's face. She looked like she was melting. Her features sagged. She grew even paler, and her shoulders hunched as Mitch continued speaking to her. A soft moan came through the speakers that were wired to the microphone attached to her collar. She began to sway slightly from side to side.

After a moment, Mitch backed away, and Ariel seemed to pull herself together. Taking a shaky breath, she shuffled the papers in her hands and began speaking in a quavering voice.

"Moving on, I will now share a reading from *The Little Prince*," she said. "'Water may also be good for the heart. . . .'"

The quote didn't seem to have anything to do with what was going on, but everyone looked relieved that things were moving forward again. "'The stars are beautiful, because of a flower that cannot be seen,'" Ariel continued reading. Then, suddenly, she stopped. Several of the groomsmen darted in to support her as she swayed dangerously to one side, but she waved them away. She began reading again. Unfortunately, she started from the beginning.

Three more times Ariel started her reading, lost her place, and began again. Finally, she stopped—and dropped like a stone. After so many false alarms, the groomsmen had grown careless. No one caught her. The thud as she hit the ground was projected by her microphone to wonderfully dramatic effect. Everyone froze.

"Oh God, what do I do? Keep shooting? Is that right?" said a relative with a video camera, addressing the question to anyone at all.

"Of course you keep shooting," said Sarah. "Memories are made of this."

Kristie screamed. All attention switched firmly back to

the bride. Guests leaped up to support her. Bridesmaids scattered in a flurry of flowers and ruffled skirts. Mitch backed slowly away. Kristie, slumped in the supporting arms of her maid of honor, looked down at her collapsed officiant.

"How could this happen?" she gasped. "I just don't understand how this could happen."

Finally, a doctor among the guests actually thought to check on the condition of the fallen Ariel. "She's all right. Please don't worry," he said, though no one appeared to be worried. They were all far too busy with Kristie. The doctor helped Ariel to a chair.

"I want to finish the ceremony," she insisted weakly. "Their souls must be united."

I elbowed Sarah, who was doubled over with laughter. Ten minutes later, with the support of two groomsmen, Ariel rose from her chair and slowly made her way back to the ceremony site and to Kristie, who stood waiting there, pale but determined.

"I can do this," Kristie said to her mother, who was fanning her with a copy of the program. "Where's Mitch?"

Mitch was over near the ornamental fountain, chatting to the prettiest of the bridesmaids.

Kristie's lips thinned a little. "Baby, we're ready to start again," she called. Mitch looked up.

"It's about time. What's the holdup here? Can we get this show on the road?"

Ariel started reading her quote from *The Little Prince*.

"Skip to the vows already!" groaned Sarah. "No way is she going to make it. Look at her. Oh, no. She's stopped reading already. I can't stand it."

We watched as Ariel turned very slowly toward Kristie. "I am so sorry, my dear," she said politely, and vomited down the front of Kristie's Reem Acra gown.

Kristie looked down. Her lips moved, but no sound came out.

Then it did.

"Get it off me!" she screamed. "Get it off me! Get it off! Get it off!"

She kept repeating this as four of the groomsmen lifted her up, her body forming a crucifix shape, head lolling back to give us one last view of her mascara-stained face as she was carried from the scene. Mitch, fully present at last, followed. Both bride and groom were still wearing their body mikes, so we heard Kristie's hysterical weeping and Mitch's curses for several more minutes until the doors of the bridal room shut behind them.

Three women with walkie-talkies had now rushed to the scene and stood looking with blank expressions at the bride's abandoned shoes covered in vomit, the stunned guests, and the gagging ring bearer. This was not in the planning guide. Ambulance sirens were heard in the distance.

"Wow," said Sarah.

*O*ne month later, Kristie came to pick up her pictures. Surprisingly, they didn't look too bad. After an hourlong wait while the bride, the officiant, and the wedding site were all scrubbed, the vows had actually happened. They were very short. Then the officiant left in an ambulance and the reception played itself out, with everyone trying hard to forget what had just taken place. I tried to piece together a book of pictures that documented the fiction that this marriage was off to a glorious start. It seemed like the least I could do.

Kristie arrived beaming. She hugged me and handed me a huge purple orchid plant. "Wasn't the wedding a dream?" she said. "I'll always remember it as a perfect day. And you were perfect, too, Claire."

Kristie's rose-colored glasses must have been stuck on with Super Glue. But perhaps that was a good thing, I thought, if she was to live with Mitch. She hugged me again and left with her pictures.

It was almost a year later that I met a coworker of Kristie's who came to talk with me about photographing her own wedding. She was anxious to tell me the whole story.

"That lady doing the wedding," she said, "you know, the crazy one? Well, she got Kristie and Mitch's letters mixed up with someone else's letters, and when Mitch told her what she had done, she had a total nervous breakdown. Can you imagine being so embarrassed you, like, throw up all over someone? Other than that, though," she continued, "it really was a perfect wedding. Can you believe they got divorced already?"

2

Postmodern Panty Raid

*J*ust give me your damn underwear," snarled the bride. She had the last holdout among her bridesmaids up against the wall. "Come on. I need them."

There was no response.

"OK, listen, you," she snapped. "Everyone else did it. It's your turn. I need those underpants, now!"

Still no response.

The bride abruptly changed her tactics. "I don't understand you. Honey," she murmured forlornly, "you're supposed to be my friend, none of the other ones fit right, and this is supposed to be my special day. My really superspecial day!" One lone tear spilled over and ran down her cheek.

"The makeup," warned Bruno the stylist.

She stopped crying immediately and settled for sniffling.

The bridesmaid watched her, unmoved. "My underwear is staying right where it is."

I backed into a corner to try to avoid becoming collateral damage, wondering for the tenth time since I arrived,

Why am I here? Is there any way I can leave right now? For a wedding photographer, these are questions that come up pretty regularly. But here I was, along with Sarah, who had collapsed on a chair in the corner twenty minutes ago and hadn't moved since. Sarah has a way of getting out of the line of fire before complete mayhem sets in at a wedding. And this one was complete mayhem. A crew of exhausted makeup artists, hairstylists, and bridesmaids littered the room. All of us were at the mercy of a bride who was clearly not given enough time-outs as a child.

Finally, the last of the seven bridesmaids was bullied into submission. Stripping off her tiny flesh-colored thong, she balled it up and, flinging it at the bride, cried, "I hope you're happy now." She vanished into the bathroom, slamming the door behind her.

"Perfectly," the bride purred. "But why couldn't she have just given it to me right away without making such a fuss about it? This drama queen stuff is exhausting." She slipped into her purloined undies. "See, no lines now."

"There were none there before," shouted the panty-deprived bridesmaid from behind the bathroom door.

"Let's just move on, shall we?" said the bride sharply. "Come on, everybody. This is supposed to be a happy day. Let's have a wedding. What are we waiting for? Smiles, everyone!"

The temperature is 102 degrees today, and for the past two hours I have been stuck in this knickknack-filled room at a Napa bed-and-breakfast. I want a cold shower and a beer. I want to go home. But when you live in San Francisco and are trying to make your living as a photographer, you do what you have to do to pay the rent. I take a look over at Sarah. She's usually fairly easygoing, but I don't mess with her when she gets irritated, and this bride is driving her crazy. She's slumped over with her head in her hands. It would be great if she could at least try to pretend she's enjoying her work, but I'm scared to mention it. I don't give her a lot of direction. I once asked her to please drive just a little faster, and she came within inches of killing a pedestrian.

I hired Sarah about a year ago. Business was flourishing, and I was getting busier all the time. I felt like one of those high-powered entrepreneurial women that you see in magazines. So I decided to indulge in the luxury of some help. Someone to carry my camera bags, run back and forth to the lab, think of me as a combination mentor and friend. Perhaps even provide a little company during the dull parts of an eleven-hour shoot. It sounded great.

In response to my ad, Sarah strode in. "Hello, here is my resumé and these are four letters of recommendation. I am familiar with medium format, thirty-five millimeter, all lighting systems, all Microsoft applications, and I am an excellent and reliable driver. I speak Spanish, French, and just a little Russian. I think you will find me to be a highly qualified assistant, and," she added, "I am comfortable in all social situations." She was also beautifully dressed and about five inches taller than me.

"Well, that just about covers it," I said. "Is there anything else I should, ah, ask you?"

"I am excellent with dogs and children," she smiled.

Half an hour later, she had finished interviewing me and had agreed—on a trial basis—to see if she could put up with my shortcomings. She was efficient and talented. She understood all those technical gizmos that had been baffling me for years. In the space of fifteen minutes she redesigned my pricing structure and told me how to make my computer stop invoicing everybody twice. Unless things go wrong, we do very well together. But Sarah has a couple of quirks. She does not like prima donnas, and she needs to eat at regular intervals. Today I have forgotten to bring any emergency energy bars, and the bride thinks the world exists to please her. So I'm keeping my distance, and my ace assistant is temporarily no help at all. Meanwhile, at a nearby winery, 250 guests have been broiling in the midday sun for just over two hours. My cell phone rings.

"Do you want the body count?" It's the wedding coordinator. "We've got two in the over-sixty-five crowd down with heatstroke. The flower girl is naked in the ornamental fountain. Oops, no, wait, now she's being pulled out of the fountain. Boy, listen to that kid scream. Isn't that just lovely?" There is a note of desperation in her voice.

"I'm battling it out on the front lines here," she says. "The flowers have wilted. The bridegroom is getting drunk with the bride's stepfather. It's a mess. What are you guys doing? When the hell are you going to get over here?"

I've never heard her sound this way. This is a woman who can calmly deal with a group of drunken fraternity brothers throwing bridesmaids into a pool. I've even seen her perform the Heimlich maneuver on an elderly guest who was choking on an olive, without wrinkling her Armani suit. Things must be really bad over there.

"I'll find out, I promise," I tell her. "I'll call you right back with an update." I go and check in with Bruno.

"The updo is a disaster," he says with a shrug. "She kept bending over to try on all those underpants, and now it's all flopped over onto one side."

"It's ruined," moans the bride, looking in the mirror and trying to push her hair back into place. "Bruno, help me. Look at this. I can't go out there like this. I swear, Bruno, if you don't fix this, I'm not going. I'm just not."

"Twenty minutes," says Bruno with perfect calm. The Zen Stylist is how he bills himself. "You should meditate, Claire," he says, smiling serenely at me. "That way you wouldn't get so tense. My yoga practice keeps me centered and relaxed in all situations. Of course, I chant, too."

"You didn't look like you were chanting when I saw you washing down that Xanax with a shot of vodka earlier," I mutter close to his ear. Bruno gets busy repairing the damage.

I call the coordinator back.

"Great," she says. "You know who they'll blame? Oh, sure, I'm the one who's supposed to keep it all running smoothly, even if the bride is a raving maniac. Go ahead, just blame me. You're lucky all you have to do is take the pictures. Your biggest problem is a bride with a spot on her nose, right? But they know you can photograph them with a double chin or a wide rear end, so they never give you a hard time. Oh, no, everyone is always polite to the photographer."

"Hey, don't shoot the messenger, OK?" I say. "I'll move things along as fast as I can."

I make my way over to Sarah. Someone, I notice, has brought her a large glass of lemonade and a damp washcloth for her forehead. I don't know how she does it. She can generate more sympathy in five minutes than I can get in all of a long hard day. All she has to do is look up and murmur the word "headache" in a pathetic tone of voice, and people will scurry to help her. If I did that, they'd just ask me if I was sure I was still well enough to do my job. I maneuver her out into the hall.

"Headache any better?"

"A bit," she nods.

"OK then, could you please just get over to the winery and see if you can get a few shots of whichever of the older guests haven't passed out yet, and maybe some flower shots of anything that still looks slightly fresh? Oh, and can you try to dry off the flower girl and get some sort of a picture of her that her mother will like? Actually, you'd better see if the groomsmen will get together for a shot before they get any drunker, too, and maybe get a shot of the bride's stepfather now because I think he's starting to fight with the groom's dad, OK?"

Sarah looks like her headache might be coming back. "You know you always make me do the hard stuff, right? You know you're just sending me because it's a total mess over there?" Just then we hear a wail of distress. It sounds like the redo on the hair may not be going too well.

"Do you really want to stay here?"

Sarah laughs and heads for the door. "I'm on it, chief."

I'm back on the phone to the coordinator. "I've sent

Sarah over to take some pictures," I say. "Maybe that will distract everyone."

"Oh, sure," she says. "Let's see, the groom has now had six shots of tequila with the groomsmen. The bride's mother won't talk to her husband because he thought it was funny to pick up the microphone and tell all the guests that his stepdaughter is an idiot. The groom's grandmother fainted from the heat and is no longer here. The white roses are all brown, and the harpist went home twenty minutes ago. I really don't think Sarah can fix this."

Suddenly the hall is full of bridesmaids. The bride is finally satisfied, and we are leaving. "We're on our way!" I tell the coordinator, and run to grab my camera bag. At the door, the bride stops.

"Hey, shouldn't we do some portraits of me alone before my makeup gets all runny? We have time, right?" Everyone looks at me.

"Afterward would be much better," I tell her. "We can do lots of pictures later."

What I don't tell her is that from behind I can clearly see the outline of a tiny flesh-colored thong marring the perfect line of her Vera Wang gown.

3

Turning Twenty

$\mathcal{I}$ hadn't planned on being a photographer at all. I spent the last years of my teens at Juilliard hoping to get the training I needed to become the only thing I'd ever wanted to be, an actress. After two years in the Juilliard hothouse of anxiety and ego, I was evicted from school with barely a shred of desire to work in theater left intact. I spent all of my twenties recovering.

My formal theater training had been a nightmare. Quite apart from the fact that my teachers told me I lacked talent and had a lisp that might require restructuring my jaw, I couldn't get over my feeling of complete foolishness whenever I was required to do most of the things that my acting teachers requested, such as reciting *Antigone* while pretending that I was on a tightrope or letting the entire class watch while I did things I would normally only do in private. Everyone else seemed completely comfortable speaking Shakespeare while pretending to swing from a trapeze. They were also more talented, thinner, more attractive, more experienced—I was a virgin, for goodness sake, what was wrong with me?

I did get some advice. One acting teacher told me to read *Madame Bovary*. I went home immediately and read it like a Bible. Was the answer in there? I loved the book, but no one thought my acting got any better. Another teacher told me that I should get more deeply in touch with the grit of life. Think dirt, blood, feces, I was told. I tried. The movement teacher told me to free my body from the waist down. I tried that, too. My roommate tried to help by giving me a hit of acid for my eighteenth birthday. That would loosen me up! I had a long chat with some squirrels in Central Park and watched the meat at a deli counter come alive and crawl away. No major changes followed.

Since I was very young, I had dreamed of the parts I most wanted to play. Though we did many of the plays I loved, I didn't get the roles I had fantasized about. I was almost always cast as the maid. I learned that there are maids in a surprising number of plays. I watched Kelly McGillis playing Masha in *Three Sisters*. I was the maid. And then she was Viola in *Twelfth Night*. Oh, no, not Viola! I'd been memorizing that part since I was fourteen. Turns out there's a maid in *Twelfth Night,* too. I watched Elizabeth McGovern play every role that called for a tall, willowy ingenue and saw Kevin Spacey finesse his way through the politics of the place as if he'd been doing it all his life. I did do a brief and disastrous turn as Cleopatra, feeling squeamish when I kissed the look-alike son of a famous movie star who was playing Mark Antony and who unfortunately had a huge cold sore on his lip. I then had to faint into my waiting women's arms.

"He goes forth gallantly," I said, watching my retreating Mark Antony and feeling, as usual, like an idiot, thinking, *Get me the hell out of here.*

Things got worse. My accent, the product of a childhood spent in three different countries, was unacceptable. The august and terrifying voice teacher told me I sounded like a bleating lamb. My singing was nonexistent. The head of the drama department dismissed the questions I asked in his Shakespeare seminar as provincial. I was told that my chances of ever working in the American theater were slim to none. Unfortunately, I was still a long way from being able to say, "Take that, you pretentious twits," and walk out. So I stayed and believed everything they told me.

Then there was the whole sex thing. Though I thought it might help me somehow in my acting, not to mention the freeing up of my lower body, I didn't want to sleep with anyone I'd met so far. No one else seemed to have the same problem. Students were sleeping with teachers. Students were sleeping with each other. Everyone seemed to be having a fine time, except me. It wasn't that I wouldn't have been perfectly happy to join in, but I wanted true love.

We did a production of *The Crucible.* I looked through the script. No maid! My luck was turning. For weeks, a young guest director had us meet in a rehearsal room to improvise. You are a group of repressed young women meeting at night in the woods, he would tell us. Work yourselves into a frenzy. So we did. I faked frenzy as best I could and felt not only stupid but suspicious of this odd man who seemed to be enjoying watching our frenzy a little too much. "Don't forget," he'd say, "there would have been a strong erotic component."

When the play was finally cast, I had one line. As the ancient grandmother who is led away to be killed, I complained that I had not yet had my breakfast. I tried for touching, or at the least pathetic. I was told I failed miserably. At the end of my first year, the teaching staff said I could come back for a second but should consider myself on very shaky ground. This did nothing for my self-confidence or my acting. I limped home for the summer.

My mother, who had grown up in a very different time and remembered Club Med as thatched huts on beautiful beaches and the playground for elegant Europeans on vacation rather than an extended-spring-break club for Americans looking to drink as much as possible and get laid, thought that a trip by myself would be just the thing to give me a good rest and a break from school. So when I came home from school bruised and demoralized, she sent my sad eighteen-year-old self off to two weeks at a Club Med.

I had always been a reader, so my stock of knowledge was in many ways extraordinarily broad. I had traveled a great deal from a very early age, spoke several languages, and lived alone in New York. But my practical knowledge of life was pretty low. I was, in fact, completely naive and absolutely sure that I was not. A dangerous mix. In my case it meant that I spent two weeks misunderstanding things simply by being too ignorant to know what was going on. I tried Ecstasy and woke up on the beach at 5:00 A.M. with no memory of how I'd gotten there, happily agreed to judge a contest and then realized it involved comparing the lengths of several men's erect penises, and completely misunderstood one woman's offer to indoctrinate me into the pleasures of intimate female company. I just thought I was making a great new friend. Another couple's efforts to show me how much fun group sex could be fizzled when I missed the point so entirely that I think they were embarrassed to have to explain to me why they were suggesting that we all climb onto the bed together. Finally, the group I shared a table with at meals announced one night to the whole room that I was the only virgin at the Club and asked if anyone wanted to help me out of my predicament. I came home mortified, hungover, no happier, and even less confident than before. My mother, a wise and lovely woman who loved me and my brother and sister to distraction, told me that life was short and that to waste time being unhappy was crazy. I knew she was right, but I didn't know how to be happy.

I made it through one more year of school and was asked to leave. I can't comment on my lack of talent, but given my self-consciousness, they were probably right. The life of an actress was not for me, though it took me a few more years of frustration to be convinced of that. Now, looking back, it seems I dodged a bullet.

Since the school had told me not to cut my hair, the minute I left I cut it down to one inch of black spikes. I started auditioning and, within a few months, got a small role in a play that got me my equity card and a weekly paycheck. I figured this was the beginning of my life in the theater. When the play closed, I started auditioning again, but this time I was not so lucky. I spent many months going from one audition to the next without so much as a second look from a casting director. Most of the time I never even got to read a line. It seemed my acting career was over almost before it had begun. Pretty soon my meager savings were entirely gone, and I was thoroughly miserable.

I got a job manning the door at a trendy bar. This would, I told myself, let me look for my next acting job during the day—which amounted to a few pointless auditions for television commercials. Auditions like the one for a shampoo ad. For that one I stood in front of a row of men in chairs and pretended to be shampooing my almost bald head while I recited, "Mmmmm, feels so good, and smells good, too," with great enthusiasm. I realized that I was not crazy to feel ridiculous. This *was* ridiculous. I would probably never be cast as Viola, and I was wasting time. In my family, wasting time was a sin.

I stopped auditioning. I wanted to be happy again. I wanted an adventure, and I found one. I fell in love. Happiness indeed. Forget everything else. This was joy. Unfortunately, joy happened to be a very charming, extremely witty, my-idea-of-perfectly-handsome bartender. One who drank too much, snorted too much cocaine, and slept with everything that moved. Good choice. But you'll perhaps excuse me if I say we had a wonderful time. Anyone who's ever been in love for the first time with a good-looking, clever, romantically dissolute, and slightly dangerous person will know what I mean. It was not wise. It was not sensible. It was divine. For the better part of a year we saw very little daylight. I'd meet him at his bar when he closed up for the night and we'd head out to dance, drink at after-hours clubs, eat steak and eggs at 4:00 A.M., and go home to make love.

It took me longer than it should have to understand that

my big fish was swimming in a very small pond. In fact, he wasn't really anything out of the ordinary when viewed in the light of day. Even through very bleary eyes, I eventually spotted the cracks in the facade. After that, it was a steady slide into messiness, lies, other people's underwear in his bed, too much drinking and snorting, and every kind of casual cruelty. But awareness doesn't mean that you don't break your heart. It just adds some self-derision to the mix. Never one to do things by halves, I did heartbreak for about five years. I know. That sounds excessive to me, too. Perhaps it was just the culmination of a series of disappointments. No acting and no love. I would now spend far too much time taking foolish risks and generally punishing myself for being so silly as to aspire to either.

But good came from all this, and I was lucky. I managed not to injure myself physically or mentally while taking horrendous chances for a few years, and then I found what I was looking for. I had started fooling around writing a book about a character who was a photographer. Why not take the character's pictures myself and put them in the book? A friend helped me buy a camera, and I started learning. I loved it from the start. Really loved it. When I was photographing, it felt like dancing. I lost all sense of myself, as opposed to my efforts as an actress, when I had felt so constantly awkward and self-conscious. The real beauty of it was there were no auditions. I needed no one's permission to do the thing I wanted to do. My looks, my voice, my whole uncomfortable self were immaterial. I could work alone. I could photograph things I cared about. I could move lightly through the world with just my camera.

I bought an open-ended Air France ticket that would let me travel around Africa for as long as my limited money would hold out, packed as much film as I could afford, and went away from everything. I felt like my life was beginning. A bit late in the day, but better late than . . . Well, you know what I mean.

4

Queen for a Day

$\mathcal{M}$yra flew through my door like a balloon with a puncture. She sputtered around the room making a lot of noise that sounded like "hello how are you and oh my those are a lot of steep steps you have there and I really just can't breathe is this all your own work up here on the walls?" Finally, she deflated on the couch. After catching her breath and settling her generous bottom—squeezed tightly into embroidered stretch denim—more comfortably into the cushions, she opened a leopard print bag the size of a small suitcase and pulled out a manila folder.

"I have a vision for my daughter's wedding," she said. She tapped her right temple with a finger half-covered by an amethyst ring. "It's all up here. And once I get a vision, there's no stopping me until it comes to life."

I knew it was probably best to raise my hands and back away slowly. But it was a quiet Thursday afternoon, and there was nothing urgent I had to do. So I said, "Tell me all about it."

Somewhere in the bottom of her bag, her cell phone began to play the Mexican Hat Dance. "Work, they never leave me alone," said Myra, rolling her eyes. She ignored the phone and started talking.

"My daughter, Altea, lives in New York," she said. "She has asked me to arrange all the details of her wedding." The Mexican Hat Dance seemed to be getting louder.

"Would you like to answer that?" I asked.

"Oh, just ignore it. I always do," said Myra. "We are inseparable, my Altea and I. If she had her way, she'd still be at home with me. I practically had to push her out of the house to make her go."

It seemed odd—then—that, if mother and daughter were so close, Altea had chosen to move as far away from her mother as was possible while still living in the same country.

"My daughter has agreed to place her wedding entirely in my hands," Myra continued. "Obviously, this is a wise decision. She has made only one request. She would like you to photograph her wedding. You photographed her friend Michelle's wedding, and Altea liked the pictures. Therefore, she has asked me to hire you. I would, of course, have preferred that the choice be mine, but I have agreed to this request. I am hiring you against my better judgment. Please don't be offended by this. I simply feel Altea should have left all the details up to me." She paused and looked at me for a moment. Perhaps I looked worried, because she patted my arm reassuringly.

"Please don't be concerned," she said kindly. "I will provide you with notes and instructions." She opened the folder that lay on her lap. "Here is a contract I have prepared for you. Please sign it in all the places I have highlighted in yellow."

"Well, actually, I have my own contract," I told her. "You just need to sign it in one place, and we're all set." There was a brief silence. Myra took my contract carefully in two fingers as though it might bite her and slipped it into her bag.

"I'll get back to you," she said.

I wasn't sure I'd hear from Myra again, or if I wanted to, but several days later, I received an envelope in the mail. Inside was my contract, as well as a series of attachments. Myra was worried about liability issues. The itemized list of possible trouble that might befall me at Myra's home did not inspire confidence. I telephoned her.

"Do you need me to initial each of the possible problems?" I asked.

"Absolutely, you never know what might happen," she said. "At Altea's cousin's wedding the caterer tripped and fell down the stairs. He completely shattered two vertebrae. He's partially paralyzed now, and that's no joke. That could happen to you, too. I also have a swimming pool, and people do drown, you know. There is also the issue of the animals."

"Animals?"

"I have a dog and a cat. Both have been known to bite." She paused as another terrible possibility came to mind. "You don't have allergies, do you?"

"No, no allergies."

"Oh, thank goodness. But still, car accidents can happen, and food poisoning. It is best to be prepared. Do please initial each clause, and be sure to add a signature at the end where it says I am not liable for any accidents I may have forgotten to specify."

I initialed them all, but I couldn't help thinking that she had neglected all the problems that were far more likely to occur. I would have been happy to get a little protection from boredom, irritation, bad music, or spoiled children.

*T*hrowing a wedding at home can be daunting. For Myra, it was a nightmare. The closer the wedding came, the more she panicked, and the team of vendors she had selected was plunged into wedding hell. I received twenty-three e-mails from Myra, clarifying and refining her expectations of me. The caterer, one of the best and most experienced in the business, called me a couple of weeks before the wedding.

"I can't take any more of this," he groaned.

"What's the trouble?"

"She's driving me nuts. She's changed the menu four times and had me out to her place for three site visits, and she called this morning to say she wants the food to match the color scheme for the flowers."

"What color are they? I asked. "You could think of this as an artistic challenge."

"That's not the point!" He sounded frustrated.

"Sorry," I said, "I just thought it might be kind of fun for you to try something different."

"Different! Have you ever tried creating an entire meal in jewel tones? Have you?"

I was delighted when the day finally arrived. It was like

going to the dentist to have a painful tooth pulled. You know this part won't be fun, but at least it will put an end to the constant nagging irritation.

I tried to prepare Sarah as we drove to the wedding. "This lady is a maniac," I told her. "We're going to need to help this girl and try to get her the sort of pictures she wants without her mother getting in the way. And for goodness sake, don't trip over anything or get bitten by the dog."

"Wow, she really got to you, didn't she?"

"No, she didn't get to me. I'm just trying to help you, and you are not helping by not listening," I said.

Sarah laughed.

"OK," I said. I was laughing now, too. "I know it sounds nuts. But listen, the food is probably in jewel tones, so get some food shots in color, please."

"Jewel tones? Are you serious?"

"Dead serious," I said. "And you need to watch out for the edge of the pool. Myra says it's very easy to fall in."

After fifteen more minutes of warnings and suggestions, Sarah closed her eyes and pretended to sleep the rest of the way.

*M*yra shared her enormous home with a small man who was her husband. He may have started out quite small—there's no way to be sure—but certainly life with Myra had made him no bigger. At this point in their life together he was almost invisible. He greeted me at the door and then quickly backed up against the wall as our hostess appeared. Myra was wearing a dress that was designed for a woman twenty years younger and fifty pounds lighter. Having squeezed herself into this long, strapless pink tube, she would now be immortalized in my photographs as a fancy sausage.

"Do you think she believes she looks good in that?" Sarah murmured.

"You have to admire her courage," I said.

"I do?"

An air of tension had entered the room with Myra. She was clutching one side of her head and looked distressed.

"Do you have a headache?" I asked.

"Oh," she moaned. "It's terrible. That fool of a hairdresser has burned my ear."

Poor Myra. No matter what disasters you list on a contract, life can always come up with another one.

Sarah and I took a look around. The inside of the house was as tightly packed as Myra's dress. The interior was a monument to keeping the American economy healthy. No expense had been spared, and good taste did not interfere in any way. We slid past the grand piano and went outside to find the bride. The descent from the house to the gardens below was a series of terraces separated by steep wooden steps. Each terrace had its own distinctive flourish—a fountain, a statue, a gazebo, a marble hot tub, and, finally, a bride. Altea looked dangerous. Everything about her was sharp; her elbows, her nose, her collarbones, even her finely arched eyebrows. To hug Altea would be to risk serious bodily harm. She wore a heavily beaded wedding gown, an air of privilege, and a scowl. She also wore the longest veil I had ever seen. It was of fine cream-colored lace embroidered with pale pink flowers, and it stretched out behind her like a sail. As we approached, the veil was being adjusted by a stylist. "I don't want it to move an inch. Is that clear?" said Altea.

"Believe me, this would survive a direct hit from a tornado," said the stylist.

"Just make sure," Altea snapped back. If Altea had let her mother plan her wedding, it was not because she didn't know how to stand up for herself.

"I see serious entitlement issues," said Sarah.

"I see a very long day," I said.

Altea was attended by eight blond bridesmaids. With their identical French twists and strapless dresses in pale champagne silk, they were frighteningly alike. I tried to find some distinguishing characteristics.

"Clones," said Sarah.

"Hello, everyone," I said.

Altea had no time for greetings. "I want to do these pictures right after the ceremony," she said, handing me a typed list. "I'd like to have the photography impose on the flow of the day as little as possible."

"So would I," I said, smiling.

She did not return my smile. "We'll do them on that patch of lawn over there. I checked the angle of the sun at four fifteen, and it will be fine."

I looked at the list. "That's quite a long list."

"I have allotted you fifteen minutes for pictures," said Altea, as though she were offering me a gift. I tried one more smile.

"Taking forty pictures in fifteen minutes will be quite hard," I said. Bride and bridesmaids stared at me blankly.

"Fifteen minutes leaves very little time for each picture, you see? And some of these groups are very big."

No one said a word.

"I'm sure you can see this won't really work. We can't make all your poor relatives run around that fast, right?" I was beginning to babble.

"Is there a problem?" Altea asked. I thought I had just explained the problem.

"Altea," I tried, "the pictures will probably take a little longer than you have planned for. Can we perhaps do a few of them now, or allow a little extra time?"

She looked at me a moment. "No. I do not plan to miss my cocktail hour, and I don't want to take pictures now."

I tried to lighten the atmosphere a bit. "Well, not to worry, you won't miss your cocktail hour, because we'll probably all be drinking by the time we get through this list anyway."

The silence that followed was broken by one of the bridesmaids.

"Is she allowed to say that? Tell her you're not paying her to party, Altea!"

$\mathcal{M}$yra found me in the garden, where I was busy taking photographs of the bride's flowers. A bouquet can't tell me how it wants to be photographed. It's a nice change sometimes.

"Nothing's working," she said miserably. "The caterer is hiding from me. I'm so disappointed with everything he's done, and I can't find him anywhere to tell him so. Also, that florist, who used to be a friend of mine, has kept none of her promises to me. None!"

"The flowers are lovely," I told her. "Look at this bouquet. And the arrangements in the house are wonderful."

"Maybe," said Myra, "but the groomsmen are so badly brought up. They don't seem to have any manners, and those bridesmaids are completely ignoring poor Altea. Nothing is going right. I simply cannot take much more. Thank God you're here. Only you have not let me down."

"Everything looks lovely. I'm sure Altea is happy," I said. I figured it wouldn't be long before I was on Myra's hit list myself.

*B*y late afternoon, Myra had calmed down and decided she liked the flowers after all, and her ear was practically back to normal size. The bridesmaids were now "such angels, Claire. I tell you. They love my Altea." We were ready to have a wedding.

The groom stood waiting on a raised platform decorated with pots of jewel-toned hydrangea and tulips, and the ceremony was starting right on time. The bridesmaids carefully threaded their way down the sixty-four narrow wooden steps that zigzagged down from the uppermost deck to the lawn. It was a torturous course, almost impossible to navigate in long gowns and very high heels. There was one tense moment when a stiletto got wedged between two steps, but it was pried loose, and all eight bridesmaids made it to the bottom unscathed. The quartet struck up Pachelbel's Canon, and the bride appeared high up on the topmost deck. It was Myra's vision. "Altea will appear like a princess and float down the steps on her father's arm," she had told me. For the first ten steps or so, that was exactly how it went.

"Myra must be in heaven," I said to Sarah.

"She's not down yet," said Sarah.

With a long lens on my camera, I photographed the bride, smiling serenely, as she went gliding past the flowering bushes that bordered the path. She and her father were moving at a pretty good pace when suddenly Altea's head twisted and jerked sharply backward. Fighting to keep her balance, Altea clutched frantically at her father's arm. Taken by surprise, he stumbled and dropped from sight behind the bushes.

"Whoops," said Sarah. Someone in the crowd said, "Where's he gone?" A moment later, he popped back up above the bushes like a jack-in-the-box. There was applause from the crowd, and Altea's father gave a mock bow. Altea was not amused. Then the pair was in motion again.

Whatever had gone wrong, they seemed to have sorted it out. As they rounded the first hairpin turn of the steps, the guests could finally see the bride in all her glory. I noticed that her lips seemed a little tight and her father was limping slightly, but they were looking pretty good. Five more steps down, and things went wrong again. Altea's head was yanked so sharply to the left that she was suddenly bent over sideways. "It's the veil," said someone in the crowd. "It's caught on the steps." Stretched out for fifteen feet behind Altea, her delicate veil had become firmly wedged between two of the steps. Her father yanked at the fragile lace. Altea rocked backward. There were gasps from the crowd, but I definitely heard a few giggles mixed in as well.

I looked over at Sarah. I had sent her off to stand near the groom to photograph his expression as he watched his bride come down the steps. She waved happily. Altea's father was getting desperate to free his daughter. With the veil now balled up in his arms, he put all his weight behind one mighty tug. He succeeded, but unfortunately his efforts left the tiara hovering over Altea's left ear. A large section of her intricate hairdo now dangled over her nose. She snarled. Even from down below it was clear that the bride was saying some very unladylike things to her father.

"She's gonna hit him," Sarah was back beside me. "Just you watch. That little princess is about to slap her daddy."

But Altea looked down at the many watching eyes below and clearly thought better of it. She straightened her headpiece, shoved most of the fallen hair behind one ear, and grabbed the balled-up veil from her father. The quartet started playing again. They were on their way. Turning, I looked for Myra. She seemed stricken, her eyes glued to the descending bride, but a few of the faces around her looked quite pleased. I photographed some gleeful expressions. Perhaps I was not the only one to whom Altea had been less than polite? At the top of the final set of steps, just when it seemed likely that Altea was going to make it to the bottom without further mishap, her heel lodged firmly in a crack and snapped off. She sat down hard, slid down four or five steps on her bottom, and came to rest flat on her back. The quartet let out a horribly false note as she landed, then lost their place in the music altogether. The crowd broke completely. One of the bridesmaids collapsed laughing on the shoulder of the nearest groomsman. The groom looked confused. "Should I do something?" he was saying. "Do I go help or stay here? What should I do?" Without Altea to tell him what to do, he seemed completely bewildered. Altea, on the other hand, knew just what to do. She scrambled to her feet, removed her remaining shoe, and tossed it into the bushes. Then, with steely composure, she grabbed her father's arm and began her final descent.

"Wow, you have to admire that," said Sarah.

"Pretty impressive," I agreed.

The quartet pulled themselves together and started to play, though not quite loudly enough to drown out Myra, who was rocking back and forth in her chair saying, "Oh, my poor, poor baby." As Altea hobbled past, she turned to her mother, smiled sweetly, and told her, "Shut up right now, Mother, everything's fine!" Then she proceeded down the aisle. The back of her dress was speckled a vibrant shade of moss green.

The rest of that wedding was a blur. I try to forget the details of truly horrible weddings. Otherwise I'd never do another. I know the family photographs were endless and miserable. Relatives kept popping off to the bathroom or to get a cocktail, and by the time they came back, half the others had gone off to find them. Altea complained constantly, and Myra decided I was not the gem she had hoped I'd be. The groom peacefully sipped mojitos with the bride's father and smiled quite happily for every picture. Somehow the meal was eaten, the cake cut, and the toasts made. Sometime close to two in the morning, I crawled off to find my car. Sarah was curled up in the backseat asleep. "I found the caterer," she said sleepily when I woke her. "We had a drink or two, and he made the best dinner. I figured you had things under control, so I took a little nap. Turned out to be a pretty good wedding after all, didn't it?" She smiled and gave a huge yawn.

"Glad you had a good time." Sarcasm is lost on Sarah. What the hell, my turn to nap. I handed her the keys. "You can drive home."

$\mathcal{I}$ was away on a much-needed vacation a couple of days after Altea's wedding when I checked my answering machine for messages.

"Claire? Claire, are you there?" It was Myra. "I need to know when the pictures will be ready. Please call me back as soon as possible."

I have a short and very simple contract, but it definitely covers the main points: how much things cost, what you get, and when you will get it. I left Myra a message reminding her that the contract allows five weeks for delivery of the finished photographs.

The next call came the following day. "Claire, I need to know exactly how big the pictures will be when I finally get them. My eyes are not what they used to be, and I cannot properly see the details in small prints. I am very concerned about this, Claire. Your contract says they will be four by six, and I'm afraid that just won't work."

I didn't check my answering machine again until I came home from my vacation a few days later. The light was blinking at me when I walked in the door. I pressed the message button and heard Myra's voice. "I've been looking at your contract, Claire. It says here that you can use pictures from the wedding in your portfolio or on your Web site. I absolutely do not want this. You know, it's horrible, lots of my friends brought their own cameras to the wedding, and now they are showing pictures from the wedding to their friends without my permission. I have written to each of these people to tell them how shocked I am that they would violate my privacy in this way."

*T*wo weeks later, I called to tell Myra her daughter's pictures were ready. She arrived to pick them up within half an hour. I had carefully wrapped and packed everything, hoping to avoid having to look at them all with Myra. There were more than eight hundred images, and I had a feeling that there would be something wrong with seven hundred and ninety-nine of them.

She called me from her cell phone at half past eight the next morning. "I am very disappointed in your work," she said. "I asked you specifically to get at least one shot of each of the one hundred and fifty guests, and I can find pictures of only thirty-three of them. I'm not angry with you, Claire, just saddened that you have let Altea down so horribly. Please understand that I am telling you this for your own good, in the hope that you will not disappoint other brides in the future."

"Thank you," I said. "I so appreciate your good advice. I do have another call on the line, so I'll need to say good-bye now." I turned on the answering machine.

That evening the telephone rang. My husband forgot to let the machine answer it. Unfortunately, he suffers from terminal honesty, so despite the fact that I was frantically waving to him and mouthing the words "I'm not here," the next thing I knew he was telling Myra that I was at home and would be right with her.

"I've made a mistake," she said. "I went back through the pictures and found that there are pictures of all the guests. I'm so happy. But I am still disappointed with the quality of the photography."

"From thirty-three guests in the pictures to one hundred and fifty. Wow, that's a pretty big difference, Myra. Well, I'm glad you found everyone. Thank you for letting me know about that."

Three days later, I was chatting with Myra again.

"I've decided to submit the pictures to some bridal magazines," said Myra happily. "I'm sure they'd be interested. Would you fax a legal photo release immediately? I just wish I didn't look so fat and worried in all of them. But I suppose I can't blame you for that, can I? Do you think it was a good wedding? Did everyone have fun? I think Altea was satisfied. I haven't heard from her at all. I did so want Altea to be happy, but it's just so hard to tell if she's happy or not. Could you tell, Claire? Do you think she was?"

5

What's in the Bag?

*W*hat's in my camera bag? Well, apart from the equipment needed to do my job, there are a few additional items.

1. Swiss Army knife. Indispensable. Uses for my Swiss Army knife include:
    a. Emergency shoe, dress, and bra adjustments. Lots.
    b. Wedding dress label removal. Almost every wedding.
    c. Trimming the ring bearer's bangs. Just once. Didn't go very well.
    d. Scraping dog poop from the bride's mother's shoe. Definitely just once. And no, I didn't do it myself. There are limits.
    e. Equipment and bag repair. Too many times to count.
    f. Opening champagne bottles. Ditto.
    g. Keeping a rabid tiger at bay. Just kidding.

2. Mild sedatives. These are for me. I don't believe in using them, but sometimes it comes down to a simple choice: sedative—good, assault charge—bad. Besides, my daughter goes to a Quaker school, and they encourage peaceful conflict resolution. I'm trying to set a good example.

3. Strong sedatives. These are for the bride. Enough said.

4. Various meds. My camera bag is starting to sound like a pharmacy. These include whatever might be needed for the members of the wedding party and their families to stop headaches, runny noses, nervous stomachs, coughing, etc.

5. Band-Aids. With pictures of Spider-Man and Dora the Explorer, and the very popular ones that look like strips of bacon. These are great for putting on the imaginary hurts of flower girls suffering from pre- and post-traumatic stress disorder and the psychological wounds inflicted by well-meaning family members. Especially effective when paired with . . .

6. Chocolate. Good for the photographer's stress disorders, too. Particularly helpful when no one remembers to ask me if I've been fed until ten minutes before I'm scheduled to leave and I'm about to faint from hunger.

7. Water bottle. If you get dehydrated—which is easy to do in hundred-degree heat when you've got forty family members to herd together for

pictures and no border collie handy—you will fall down. For obvious reasons, this is bad for your pictures.

8. Tissues. I never cry at weddings, but there's always one bridesmaid who starts weeping at the rehearsal dinner and pretty much keeps it up straight through the wedding.

9. Sunblock. Napa in the summer. Need I say more?

10. Cell phone. This one is crucial. You need to have a few people on speed dial who will understand why you are calling them at 11:00 P.M. and moaning faintly. They should be trained to say, "There, there. It will all be over soon," and make soothing noises. They should also remind you that physical violence never solved anything. This is a good time to avoid the Swiss Army knife.

That's about it. Most of these supplies have multiple uses, which is nice. The chocolate can double as a mild sedative. Band-Aids can also work for emergency dress, shoe, and bra repairs, and they're good nipple concealers. Tissues are particularly good for bra work of another kind at weddings with strapless dresses and skinny bridesmaids. The sunblock works as clown makeup for truly distraught flower girls, although this option is not popular with the bride if used pre-ceremony. Finally, the Swiss Army knife: Great for crowd control—but be careful. Someone might get hurt.

6

Point and Shoot

$\mathcal{I}$ started photographing weddings because someone I loved was dying. I had been in Manhattan for twelve years. Since coming back from Africa, I had thought of the city as my home base, the jumping-off point for trips to anywhere that opportunity or my limited financial means could take me. I explored parts of North and West Africa and spent a long period in India. I slept in a tent in the Masai Mara and watched elephants walk through our camp by moonlight. In Ladakh, trying to be polite, I drank a lot more yak-butter tea than was good for my stomach. I flew Afghan Air when it was not the best time to do so, had my flight to London diverted to Kabul, and spent two days confined to a hotel and reading the anti-American propaganda I found by my bed each evening. I went on an absurd trip to Korea with a woman who claimed she was a descendant of Abraham Lincoln and hired me as her personal photographer. She had heard that Brooke Shields was in Korea with Bob Hope and wanted to ask Brooke to play her in the movie she was writing of her life story. I was to take pictures of the two of them together. I got some great shots of Brooke Shields's bodyguards. I drove through the Atlas Mountains from Marrakech to Zagora and took some risks along the way that even I don't like to think about. I went to Poland to find and photograph my mother's childhood home and rode on horseback through a Costa Rican rain forest. I was having the adventures I had wanted.

In between trips I took Photography 101 and darkroom and photojournalism classes. I assisted many photographers who knew a great deal more than I did. Some were completely impossible—I spent hours painting their studios and getting lunch for the more senior assistants—but others took the time to show me a thing or two. I apprenticed at a photo agency and learned a lot about photography but much more about the fact that this was a business of wildly passionate egos and causes. People were willing to risk a great deal to produce images that would tell a story they felt needed to be told. I started volunteering at Human Rights Watch and looked for stories to photograph that spoke to the ideas that were important to me. Slowly, I began getting some small shows of my work and assignments for various nonprofit groups. Everything seemed right on track.

*W*hen I left New York, it was sudden and sad. My mother was terribly ill. I moved to the town where she lived, about an hour south of Manhattan, and got a job working for a popular local wedding photographer. I needed work that would let me earn some money quickly and have as much free time as possible. Highly respected as the photographer of choice among the old moneyed families, she had documented the high points in the lives of several generations of the well-to-do residents in the area. Wearing one of her trademark Laura Ashley dresses, she would go out to photograph the families, marriages, and new babies in the community. There was a wonderful sameness to it all. The ivy-covered walls of local mansions formed the backdrop for perfect family portraits: There would be a slim blond mother, a hearty father, a handsomely athletic son, a willowy daughter, and a chocolate Lab or golden retriever wearing a bandanna from the local Ivy League university. She photographed their lives with a consistency that gave her clients the security that they craved. Nothing would ever change. They would stay forever in their huge houses. Their children would grow up to be responsible and wealthy. Future generations would wear alligator shirts and attend their parents' and grandparents' alma maters. They would get married at the university chapel, get their MBA, join the country club and the PTA, and eventually inherit the mansion for themselves. Her photographs helped them to maintain their belief that the world must indeed be as secure as they thought because, after all, it looked the same in her pictures year after year.

She said she would pay me fifteen dollars an hour to photograph weddings. Handing me a medium-format camera—something I had never worked with before—she told me I would start that weekend. The camera had no light meter. "Don't worry," she said. "Bright sun you shoot f11 at 250, shade you shoot f8 at 60, dark, use flash. Here, I wrote it down for you." She handed me an index card. Then she showed me how to load the camera and told me how much film to shoot. "There," she said, "you're all set. Here are the directions to this Saturday's wedding." And so I jumped into the deep end of wedding photography.

Unbeknownst to me, restaurant work, theater training, and off-the-grid travel happened to have been the perfect training ground for wedding photography. I had learned to travel light, and surprises or sudden climate changes didn't worry me. I could act up a storm when necessary, and I handled rejection well. If a bridegroom was camera-shy, I could serve him a cocktail with one hand while taking his picture with the other. I knew how to communicate with visiting guests from at least four different countries and could continue to function even if struck by food poisoning or dysentery. Perhaps someday it would even come in handy that I didn't panic when caught up in a coup attempt or when the airplane I was in was diverted to a war zone.

In the world of my new employer, everything was always in crisis. People were lost or late. Cameras broke. No one seemed to have any idea what was going on most of the time. The business, though successful, always seemed on the verge of financial ruin. So, no matter how thin we were stretched for staff, equipment, or sanity, no client was ever turned down. This meant that on a busy weekend with perhaps six or seven weddings going on, everyone was drafted to help: her daughter, her daughter's friends, the darkroom technician, her cleaning lady. We were all shooting weddings for her. The worst part was that each and every bride assumed that my employer would be photographing her wedding personally. Not surprisingly, people were not glad to see someone else turn up. Every weekend had some sort of disaster. Two photographers would arrive at one wedding and none at another. Inexperienced photographers would think they were assisting only to find they were on their own. Whole weddings were ruined. Everyone spent a lot of time apologizing, explaining, anything but refunding money. Somehow she kept it all rolling.

In a way, what made it work was the fact that no one thought you could not do it. So you did. I photographed many, many weddings for her, and she never seemed to worry about the fact that I was, in the early days, wholly unprepared to do so. So, eventually, I stopped worrying, too—and found out that indeed I did know what I was doing. I owe her a great debt of gratitude for teaching me that the best way to convince people you know what you're doing is to behave as though you know and get to work.

I've heard she's still there. Her massive desk is littered with loving notes from satisfied clients, photographs of babies and brides, and unopened letters from the bank marked URGENT. The telephone is no doubt ringing to announce another crisis at a wedding she was supposed to be photographing an hour ago, or at the lab where an entire wedding has somehow been misplaced. As much a part of that town as ever, she never lacks for business. She may get it wrong sometimes, but she belongs to that place. She is the keeper of its history.

I worked with her for most of a year shooting weddings, trying to manage the appointments, photo shoots, album orders, and screwups. In the evenings, I scrambled to manage the disaster that was the rapid disintegration of the health of a person I adored and desperately tried to stem the tide of my own fear by denying the obvious. I learned more than I ever wanted to about morphine, regret, and the feeling of helplessness that comes with the inability to save the life of the person you love best in the world. And I learned about grace. In the process of dying, my mother taught me everything I needed to know about how to live the rest of my life—though much of it has only become clear to me slowly and over time, and some of it I still don't fully understand. Even now I can pull a book off my shelf and find a note or inscription she included when she gave it to me and suddenly realize why it was that she felt that particular book or poem was the one I needed to read. My life growing up with her had been a wonder of books and ideas, travel and possibility. If I open the *Oxford Book of English Verse* I can find dozens of poems that I heard first when she read them to me. Her death solidified what she had been showing me since I was born: Beauty is important, and life is something you must pay attention to and not waste a moment of. You must take life and run with it as far and as fast as you can, and regret only the hurt you may cause but not your mistakes. Pass up no opportunity to love, to explore a new place, to feel deeply. A passionate life is the only sort worth living. Even in the act of dying, she was the most alive person I have known.

I thought I had understood that her death was coming and knew what it meant. For all the knowing, though, I had not actually been able to think about it, had not really believed it would happen. Vaguely I had imagined that at some point I would return to New York and pick up my life there exactly where I left off. But the soul does not work that way, and when she died, the world was suddenly a different place, and I was numb.

7

Babes in the Woods

I like watching kids at a wedding. They're a barometer of the level of hypocrisy involved. They don't miss much. Watch the way the kids are treated, and you will know everything you need to about the key players at the event. Just about everyone seems to picture having a couple of cute kids at her wedding. They are on the list: dress, cake, band, cute kids. Of course, everything else is bought and paid for. The kids are expected to perform for free. Certainly it is true that many children are overjoyed by the idea of being a part of a wedding. A favorite aunt or uncle is getting married, and they will get to wear fancy new clothes and throw rose petals. There will be cake. It all sounds like a lot of fun. It's more fun when the parents have a sense of humor and reasonable expectations. It is especially fun when the bride is not looking for flawless performers sent by central casting.

No situation involving children at weddings is more fraught with difficulties than the second marriage. A mother or father remarrying and wanting her or his young children to be a part of the ceremony is asking a great deal. Though wanting to include the children and make them feel a part of this new family is understandable, the kids often get lost in the process. When Shannon and Greg married, Greg wanted to make sure that his five-year-old daughter, Hannah, would be a part of the day—but he also didn't want to be bothered. It's a lot of trouble figuring out what is best for kids, and Greg had his new life to think about. It was simplest and most convenient to leave the details of Hannah's involvement to his beautiful bride-to-be. His beloved would have his daughter's best interests in mind, he was sure. Shannon, however, was interested in Shannon, and the physical reminder of Greg's former marriage was an irritation she was being forced to pretend to enjoy.

Two days before the wedding, Hannah flew with her mother from Dallas to San Francisco and was dropped off at her father's house. Her mother kissed her good-bye and went on to Paris for a two-week vacation. I met Hannah on the day of the wedding.

"I'm the flower girl, see?" She held out a basket with a big pink bow looped around the handle. "I get to throw flowers later." She bounced up and down in her excitement. She didn't know any of the people at the wedding and was trying to stick close to her father as he tried to supervise the setting up of chairs on the lawn where the ceremony was to be. He was very busy.

"Go hang out with the big girls, honey," he told Hannah, and gave her a little push toward the house, where the women were getting dressed.

"I'll go with you," I told her, and we went off together.

"Hey, there you are, cutie pie," said Shannon when Hannah arrived at the house. "Girls, you all have to come and meet my new little daughter. Isn't she sweet?" The brides-maids gathered around and admired Hannah, who looked at her toes and fidgeted.

"I'm so glad you're here, sweetie," said Shannon. "I need your help getting me ready. You are my most special flower girl, right? Now you find a place to get comfortable, and you can watch from there, OK?" Hannah went over to sit on the bed.

"No! Oh, no, Hannah! That's my dress lying there. Can't you see that? You sat on my dress!"

"Is it OK?" whispered Hannah.

"Can't someone just turn on the TV for her or something?" said Shannon.

Hannah was put in front of the TV in the room next door.

"Sit there and don't move a muscle," said the bride's mother.

I got busy taking photographs of Shannon as she fin-ished her makeup and put on her dress. "It's so important for me to include my new daughter in this special day," she was telling me when a scream went up from the room next door. One of the bridesmaids rushed in.

"The kid lifted her dress right up over her head when I was helping her put on her tights, and now she has lipstick all down the front."

Shannon went to take a look. "You silly girl, look what you did. It's totally messed up." She scowled down at Hannah.

Hannah stood like a statue while spot remover, club soda, and various other remedies were applied to her dress. Nothing worked, and the smear of pink seemed bigger than when they started.

"Well, you'll just have to look a mess," said the bride. "I don't have time for this." She went to finish getting ready.

"Come on," I said to Hannah, "let's go find your dad."

Greg was outside with his best man. When Hannah ran to him and showed him her dress, he scooped her up in a bear hug and told her everything was going to be fine. "It doesn't even show. Don't you worry about it one little bit," he told her.

"Can I stay with you now, Daddy?" asked Hannah.

Greg looked impatient. There was still a lot to do. He put Hannah down and gave her a pat on the bottom. "Why don't you go make a picture for your mommy?"

"Which one?" said Hannah.

"Your new one, honey," Greg answered, sounding flustered. "Today your new mommy is the important one, right?"

I took her to find some crayons and paper and left her as she started drawing a picture. I lost track of her for a while after that. There were portraits I needed to do, and the guests were beginning to arrive. The next time I saw Hannah was at the ceremony.

She behaved beautifully. Walking down the aisle, throwing rose petals, and standing in line with the other bridesmaids, she was a picture-perfect flower girl.

"How about a family hug?" asked the judge who was performing the ceremony. Hannah came forward and got squashed between Greg and Shannon. She looked happy. Bride and groom headed back down the aisle with Hannah following.

"Time to go, Hannah," said a babysitter who had appeared at the end of the aisle.

"Can't I stay with my dad? I want to be at the wedding," Hannah protested.

"Weddings are for grown-ups, sweetie," Shannon told her. Hannah was swept away, protesting, by the sitter.

For the next couple of hours I was busy drifting through the cocktail hour and photographing the bride and groom with their guests. There was a long formal dinner, with many toasts. Finally, the couple rose to dance.

Hannah appeared, with the babysitter in hot pursuit. "Daddy, can I watch the dance?"

Shannon looked annoyed.

"Sure you can," said Greg.

The guests smiled; they obviously thought it was sweet.

Shannon looked at her guests and decided to smile, too. She dropped gracefully to her knees and hugged Hannah. "Of course you can stay to watch," she said. "How could we have our first family dance without you?"

Hannah watched the first dance. As Shannon left the dance floor, Hannah took her hand. "I have something for you," she said shyly, holding out a sheet of paper folded in half.

Shannon looked down at her. "Oh, Hannah, don't give me anything right now," she said. "Mommy has nowhere to put it, and she's very busy. And please don't bother your daddy, either. We're getting ready to cut the cake."

Hannah watched her walk away and went to stand by the cake.

I photographed the guests as they assembled around the cake table. Shannon and Greg arrived.

"I made something for you," Hannah said to Greg, and handed him the paper she had tried to give Shannon. He looked at it and picked up the microphone that had been left ready so the bride and groom could toast their guests after the cake was cut.

"Before we cut the cake, there is something I want to say. Today I have married one of the loves of my life. The other love is right here." He picked up Hannah. "She and I would like to present this picture to my beautiful new bride." He held up the picture for the crowd to see. Three figures stood in a garden of flowers. They were holding hands. They were all smiling. I LOVE YOU, SHANNON was written underneath. Shannon wiped away a tear. She hugged Greg. She hugged Hannah. They all cut the cake together and posed for pictures.

After the cake was cut, Hannah was given a slice and sent off to eat it with the sitter.

*L*ate that evening, a limo arrived to take Shannon and Greg away to a local hotel for the night. They were to leave early the next morning for two weeks in Hawaii. The guests lined up on either side of the driveway, ready to light sparklers as the bride and groom ran past on their way to the car. No one seemed to have remembered that Hannah might want to say good-bye. Worse, no one had thought to tell her that her father would be leaving at the end of the night and that she would be going to stay with her new grandmother for two weeks. Perhaps Greg, happy to hand off the care of his daughter to her new mommy, thought Shannon had taken care of it. If so, he was relying on thoughtfulness his new bride did not possess.

The bride and groom ran down the driveway, and Hannah came streaking after them howling, "Wait!" They stopped at the limo, and she caught up. She flung herself, sobbing, into her father's arms. "Could someone please come and get her?" Shannon said. The groom looked like he might cry, too. Shannon's mother appeared and started trying to pry Hannah loose from her father. Shannon climbed into the car and slid to the far side of the seat. People, obviously upset, began to drift away. At last the screaming child was pulled away from her father by her new grandmother and two bridesmaids. Her father blew her a desperate kiss, climbed in next to his bride, and slammed the door. As the car drove away, Hannah wriggled free from the arms holding her and raced after it. Finally, as the car vanished around the curve of the driveway, she sat down on the gravel and cried. I took a picture.

8

So You Want to Be a Wedding Photographer?

*S*arah keeps up with things. This is good, because I don't. She has an iPod and knows the names of the people singing. She knows when new restaurants open and why you're supposed to be wearing wedge heels or ballet flats. She reads whatever everybody else seems to be reading and always has something intelligent to say about it. She also reads poetry and cutting-edge political commentary. She knows all about blogs and which ones are worth reading. I don't read blogs. I don't even like the word. Anyway, who has time to read them, let alone make comments? The political ones all seem to be soapboxes to preach to the converted, and the personal ones seem like a vast wasteland of useless information. Does anyone but you really care what your cat had for breakfast? Needless to say, Sarah's small talk is current, witty, and impressively well informed. Mine is not. I read a lot, too, but I spent the last year blissfully working my way through everything ever written by Trollope, and in the evening I've been known to happily curl up with the two-volume reference guides to all the obscure bits of information in my favorite Dorothy Dunnett books.

Whenever I get a cold, I climb into bed and reread *Anna Karenina* or *The Forsythe Saga,* and there's nothing better on a rainy day than settling down on the couch to read a little Colette or maybe some Dorothy Sayers. I like poetry, too. For her last birthday, I gave Sarah a copy of the *The Rubaiyat,* a long poem by my favorite Persian poet Omar Khayyam. She said that what she'd really wanted was some new novel about a woman who gets herself off antidepressants by shopping obsessively and then falls in love with a shoe designer who makes her his muse. But I know she went home and looked at it because she made a comment a few days later about a blueberry muffin, a latte, and me singing beside her in the wilderness, and then gave me a big smile. So she'd mangled a favorite quote of mine from the book, but at least it meant she'd read it. Still, when it comes to being well informed about what's new and hot, Sarah's the one who's on the ball.

If you are obsessively reading a Victorian author that no one seems to read much anymore, can't name a single *American Idol* winner, and couldn't care less where Angelina Jolie's latest baby came from, well, you're not much good on small talk. Luckily for me, Sarah helps me out and makes sure that I don't come across as looking completely out of the loop. That's just part of why our coffee meetings are so important: Sarah has her finger on the pulse of popular culture, and she doesn't mind sharing.

Today she breezes through the door with a magazine. "Check this out while I grab a coffee," she says. She hands me a fashion magazine, folded open to an article with ten suggestions for tightening my abs by bikini season. I'm not sure what Sarah has in mind. I think my abdominals are pretty good.

"What's wrong with my stomach?" I ask her when she gets back.

Sarah looks confused. "Why, does it hurt or something?"

"I'm just wondering why you think I need this. No offense, but your stomach's not exactly flat, either, you know."

"What? Oh, forget it. You are so ridiculous sometimes. Here, just read this." She takes the magazine, flips it over, and hands it back to me.

"The Most Glamorous Professions," it says. "Check out number five," says Sarah. And there it is: wedding photographer.

"No way. What idiot came up with this list?"

"It was a survey. Seriously. Tons—well, probably a lot of people think we're glamorous, baby!"

I don't feel glamorous. It's Monday morning. We shot two weddings over the weekend. My feet hurt, and I have dark circles under my eyes. I'm wearing a T-shirt that is about ten years old, even older jeans, and my crappiest pair of black Chuck Taylor high-tops. At a pinch I'd say I feel marginally cool in a hungover, bleary-eyed, black coffee, very dark sunglasses, and "I know my clothes are old but I don't give a damn" sort of way. But glamorous? That would be pushing it.

"You know what this means, don't you?" Sarah looks serious.

"The definition of glamour changed when I wasn't looking?" I'm losing interest fast, but Sarah is not about to be deflected from her point. She ignores my witty aside, as she usually does when she's on a roll.

"It means that everybody who is not tall enough to be a fashion model, talented enough to be a rock star, charismatic enough to be Oprah, or likes fish enough to be the next Jacques Cousteau"—she jabs her finger at glamorous professions number one, two, three, and four—"will decide they want to be a wedding photographer. We have to help."

"We do? Why? I don't want to help them. There are too many of us already."

"Not help them be photographers, you idiot. Help save them from themselves. Keep them from making a terrible career choice. Save them from all this glamour."

When Sarah gets an idea, she's like a freight train. I didn't want to help. I wanted to drink coffee and read the front page of *The New York Times*. I wanted to chat with Sarah about unimportant stuff like should I get my hair cut or not—I ask her about once a month, she always says no, and we move on. I was tired.

But Sarah has a plan. "We should make a list or a quiz or something. To help people decide if they really are suited to our glamorous profession. We'll send it to the magazine and they'll publish it and we will have performed a public service. Come on, Claire. You're always going on about pro bono work and using photography to do some good. And"—here she stopped to make sure she had my full attention—"your name will be in the magazine, and that will get you more clients and you need the money." She smiles triumphantly.

She knew she had me. I always need more money, and added to my usual dismal financial standing was the fact that it was late March and I would soon need to pay federal taxes, state taxes, and sales tax—as well as face the scorn of my accountant when she realized that I had once again neglected to make any estimated payments. Needless to say, she charged $450 for that hour of scorn. Glamorous indeed.

"Okay, let's get started."

Here's how it turned out: Sarah and I had an argument. Well, sort of. Sarah doesn't have a child, and I do. I wanted to create a list based on the parallels between motherhood and wedding photography. Sarah couldn't see this at all. "I'm not talking about the technical stuff, Sarah," I told her. "I'm just coming at it from the angle of sheer physical and emotional stamina." But Sarah was skeptical. The only way you ever get Sarah to agree to anything is by hitting her over the head with a baseball bat—I'm speaking metaphorically, of course, despite certain fantasies I've had that I won't mention here. So I gave her a pen and started dictating:

1. Have you ever volunteered to chaperone a field trip? Say thirty eight-year-olds going to Chinatown on public transportation who all need the bathroom at different times, forget their coats on the train, and leave their lunches at school? Have you survived this experience with your sanity intact? Did you manage not to panic when they lost teeth (not so bad) or lost their retainers (pretty bad), or when you caught one of them licking the walls of the train station (only really bad if it's your child)? Then you'll probably be just fine trying to get ten bridesmaids out of a

limousine and onto a windy beach where the bride's updo will blow over and her bridesmaids' skin will start looking like a frozen chicken's because of the gale-force winds. Someone in this group will need the bathroom, too. And there won't be one for miles.

2. Can you remove stains from the clothing of a semihysterical child? Great. A panicked and completely hysterical bride who has just found a huge smear of makeup on her dress won't send you running off to hide.

3. Are you intimidated when someone lies down on the ground, wildly kicks her feet, turns red in the face, and screams, "I don't want to," over and over? In public? Now imagine the someone is a grown woman in a long white gown from which you have not been able to remove the makeup stain to her satisfaction.

4. Can you get an unruly child to get dressed, brush his hair and teeth, put on his shoes, and get out the door on time? Now multiply that by a room full of large, half-drunk, and boisterous groomsmen.

5. Have you thrown a birthday party for twenty preschoolers, complete with jumpy house, water balloons, and a naked dance party? If so, you qualify automatically, you're a hero, and you're ready for almost any wedding reception.

6. Will you run up a hill with a huge bag of stuff on your shoulder when someone says, "Hey,

let's go play up here now!" Kids do it for fun. Grown-ups do it for pictures.

7. Can you find a creative way to suggest that it is not very nice to be rude to your mummy and daddy who love you very much and who are paying for the nice things that you are enjoying? You can say this far less politely to a child, but a bride requires some tact.

"OK, I get it." Sarah had heard enough. "But there's one thing." I figured there would be. Sarah has trouble conceding a point without at least gaining back a little ground. "You can't say that thing about mothers."

"Why? I thought that was the whole idea."

"You have to say primary caregivers. If it's not PC no one will publish it."

We never sent the list, of course. But I think it's pretty complete. So what do you think? Interested?

9

Transportation

$\mathcal{A}$ lot of my clients like creative transportation at their wedding. I have photographed couples in all sorts of vehicles. Farm wagons decorated with pots of chrysanthemums, a Hummer with a license plate that read I ♥ YOU MINDY, horse-drawn carriages, rowboats, sailboats, paddleboats, bicycles, rickshaws, classic cars, and go-carts. There are a number of perils you learn to watch out for—black tire marks on white dresses, pants cuffs getting caught in bicycle spokes, seagull droppings on the paddleboat seats—and just as many surprises guaranteed to blindside you. Anytime you bring in a new element, it comes with risks.

When things do go wrong, you hope for clients like Roxana and Omar, my first Persian bride and groom. Since then I've learned what to expect, but at that time the world of Persian weddings was new to me. "Persian weddings are always crazy," Roxana said, looking at me very seriously with a pair of the loveliest eyes I had ever seen. Olive-shaped, dark brown, and with unbelievably long lashes, those eyes were merely the advance guard of a face and body that could stop traffic. She was a stunner. "Persians are crazy," she reiterated. "We like things that way."

So it seemed, if her husband was any example. Omar was equally attractive, and obviously aware of the fact. He had the self-satisfied air of a well-bred cat. He would call me regularly from his cell phone to offer new details about the wedding plans. He was usually driving when he called and never able to hear a single word I said back to him. We would regularly lose reception in the middle of the call, but Omar never bothered calling back. He just assumed that I knew the rest of whatever he'd meant to say and was always amazed that I had "forgotten" something from one of our previous conversations.

Both Omar and Roxana were often confused about the details of their wedding.

"Can you arrive at one?" asked Roxana.

"Sure," I said. "Is that when you'd like me to arrive?"

"I'm not sure. What do you think, honey?"

Omar looked worried. "When do you usually arrive?" he asked.

"I think three would probably be fine," said Roxana. "The ceremony is at three."

"I thought you wanted pictures of when you get ready," I said, feeling as I usually did with these two that we were operating in different time zones, if not on different planets altogether.

"Yes," said Omar emphatically, "and definitely all the

family pictures done before, because we don't want to do any afterward."

"Of course," said Roxana doubtfully, "it's hard to get Persians organized ahead of time."

"How about hiring a wedding planner?"

They looked at me in total amazement. "Why would we do that when everything is already arranged?" asked Roxana.

"I'll call you," said Omar.

Two days before the wedding, Omar called, sounding frantic. "Claire, your contract says that you come for seven hours!"

"Right, it does say that. Is everything OK?"

"No, no, no," he managed to say before the phone went dead. Half an hour later, the phone rang again. "Claire, Claire, can you hear me?"

"Yes, Omar."

"We can't possibly do everything in seven hours. What were you thinking?" I didn't really have an answer to that, so I just waited to see what would come next.

"We need eleven hours at least. Definitely."

I told him what the additional time would cost. The line went quiet. I could hear traffic noises in the background, so I knew we hadn't been cut off.

Finally, I heard a sigh, and Omar spoke again. "Claire, Claire, we signed a contract with you."

I was getting fed up. "Omar, you signed a contract for seven hours, and now you want four more. It tells you right on the contract what additional hours cost."

"Oh, fine print," he said derisively, "they always get you with the fine print."

"Who gets you, Omar?"

"You wedding people."

I hung up very gently, hoping that he would keep talking for a while before he realized that this time my phone went dead first.

An hour later, Roxana called.

"Claire." She was talking fast and rather breathlessly. "Was Omar rude to you? Tell me the truth. God, he is such a jerk sometimes. Our parents are crazy. They are making us nuts. We totally love you, you know. Omar really loves you. Really. You'll still come, right? We'll pay it all properly and all that. Omar is such an idiot. I can't believe I'm marrying such an idiot! I am going to cry, Claire, really."

"Don't cry, Roxana. Just tell me when I'm supposed to get there."

"Oh, didn't Omar tell you? He is such a jerk. Noon. Just come at noon and stay till 1:00 A.M., OK?"

"That's thirteen hours, Roxana."

"Perfect," she said happily. "That should be plenty of time."

I felt like Alice on the other side of the looking glass. "Roxana, I will be there at noon. I will stay for thirteen hours. I will shoot color and black-and-white film and try my best to give you a wonderful story of your day. Do you have any idea at all about the schedule?"

"Noooo," said Roxana thoughtfully. "Persians don't really follow a schedule. But my mother has told me she wants all color pictures, OK? But Omar and I still want mostly black-and-white and just a tiny bit of color. I have to go now because my manicurist is finally done with the other lady and I don't want to miss my turn. See you Saturday."

I heard a kiss-kiss noise, and the line went dead.

$\mathcal{I}$n the taxi on the way to the wedding, Sarah had a few questions.

"So are we shooting color or black-and-white?"

I had no idea. I hate to tell Sarah when I have no idea about something. "Both, but definitely more of one than the other."

"So when are we taking the family pictures?"

"Probably right at the beginning, but maybe sometime later."

"Well, is there a lot of family?"

"Only about a hundred and forty of the three hundred guests."

Sarah turned to look at me. "You do have a list of the family groups they want photographed, right?"

"No, no list."

Sarah was quiet for a while.

"Persians are crazy," I tried to explain.

She nodded glumly. "Maybe, but these guys are just plain nuts."

We arrived at the hotel to find Roxana's suite in a complete frenzy. There was a huge crowd. Through a cloud of steam from the industrial-strength steamer in the corner, and over the whirring of hair dryers, the howls of a distressed ring bearer, and the constant ringing of multiple cell phones, I tried to say hello to Roxana.

She was having false eyelashes applied. Tiny blobs of glue were drying on her eyelids, and a makeup artist was sticking on individual lashes with the precision of a surgeon. Roxana was talking to Omar on the telephone and drinking from a bottle of Evian water. "Hey there, Claire. Stop! I have to pee," she said. Surgery stopped. Roxana went to pee. After she sat herself back in the makeup chair and got the rest of her eyelashes stuck on, she had several frantic cell phone conversations. Relatives were stranded at the airport, her mother's girdle was missing, and a bow tie had been left at the rental store.

Finally, with Roxana dressed in a gown the size of a small tank, we made it out the door and were on our way to meet Omar on the steps of the historic old bank next door to the hotel. It was in the magnificently ornate lobby of this building that both ceremony and reception were to take place. First, we would take pictures of the 140 members of their extended family, all of whom were waiting for us along with Omar. Things seemed to be going well. I felt cautiously optimistic, right up until the moment when we rounded the corner and Sarah grabbed my arm and pointed at the lone figure of Omar on the steps. "No family," she said, rather unnecessarily. Then Roxana was running, white dress billowing and narrow five-inch heels tottering, across the remaining half block toward her beloved, and I was running after her, clicking away.

Roxana and Omar kissed, hugged, and admired each other. Finally, they turned to me expectantly and asked, "What now?"

What indeed. "Do you know where your families are?" I asked. "I thought they were all going to meet us here for pictures."

Roxana laughed. "Oh, they're never on time at weddings, you know. Don't worry about them. We'll do those pictures later. What do you want us to do now? How about we go somewhere and take lots of pictures of us?"

$\mathcal{W}$aiting at the curb was the vintage Bentley that Omar and Roxana had hired to take them on a picture-taking tour of the city. A uniformed driver stood nearby, ready to chauffeur us wherever we wanted to go. Since the families weren't there and we were in the middle of a busy midtown area, it did seem a good idea to climb in, head off to a more picturesque spot, and get started on some portraits. Unfortunately, this car was not designed to hold an enormous wedding dress, a groom, two photographers with large camera bags, and a driver.

"It looked bigger in the picture," said Omar dubiously.

"I'm not getting in there in this dress," said Roxana.

"Come on, let's go take some pictures. It's just a dress, honey. Who cares?"

Sarah and I pretended to count rolls of film. We both knew that Omar had just said the wrong thing.

"Just a dress! You said you loved this dress. I thought you said you really loved this dress."

"I do. I do love the dress. We both love the dress. I'm crazy about you in that dress. That's why I want the pictures. Because I love you and the dress, see?"

"Oh, Omar. I knew you loved the dress. I love you, too. Of course we can go take pictures, but you will be careful of the dress, right?" Omar and Roxana embraced.

Sarah had her head almost buried in her camera bag. I could see her shoulders shaking.

Quite quickly it was all decided. Roxana would ride in the backseat with her dress spread out very carefully. Omar could ride back there, too, if he promised not to sit on her dress. Sarah and I and our bags would squeeze into the tiny front seat next to the driver.

Once we were all in, things began to heat up. It was a hot day, and with no air-conditioning and only those charming little side windows that open just a crack, I soon felt the sweat running down my back. Sarah was on my lap, with the two camera bags on her lap. The gearshift threatened to do me a serious injury.

"Oh, Omar, my dress is a mess," Roxana said.

"Honey, I care about your dress, but I'm suffocating here, you know. Could you just get it down off my face?"

With a few jaunty toots of the horn, we were off. At fifteen miles an hour.

"You really have to baby a beauty like this," the driver told me.

In the backseat, Omar was probably thinking somewhat the same thing. I directed us to a spot at the waterfront where one of the old piers had been restored. The site had looked so pretty from a distance a few days earlier when I had driven around scouting for locations. I had been struck by the long symmetrical line of the antique streetlamps as they receded into the fog at the end of the pier. I pictured Roxana walking toward the camera in her white dress and the stillness of the water around her. Omar would wait for her in the foreground of the picture. It would look great.

We all scrambled out of the car and gulped fresh air.

Roxana shook out her gown. "Thank God we're here. Wow, oh, this is great, Claire. I love it."

"I'm so glad."

"Let's just stay here and do lots of pictures, OK? Just don't put me back in that car," said Roxana.

Omar looked disappointed.

"What's up?" I asked him.

"I thought we were going to ride all around the city. You know, do pictures on some of the really steep hills and shots of Roxana and me running across the street. Maybe some pictures on the beach and everything."

I left Sarah to explain to Omar that his bride might have limited patience for a long car trip and took Roxana and her dress off to do some portraits. As we walked toward the pier I noticed that it was an odd color. Then it hit me. The wooden boards were coated with seagull droppings. So were the railings. There was no fog, no shade, just harsh white sunlight beating down mercilessly on bird poop and my already sweating bride. Added to this, the boards was not as close together as they appeared from a distance. In fact, the space between the boards was the perfect width to catch a tiny Jimmy Choo heel, which was exactly what happened the minute Roxana stepped sideways in a hurry to avoid a large pile of seagull droppings.

"Oh, shit. My shoe is stuck. Omar!"

"Sweetie?"

"Help me."

"OK, OK, just lean on my shoulder. We'll get you out."

"My dress, oh god, my dress. And my shoes! Omar, you're stepping on my dress. Get off me!"

"Oh, sorry. Look, I'm off your dress now, see? Don't worry. Everything will be OK. I've got you." Omar pried Roxana loose and carried her to a droppings-free spot. I took a picture of the kiss they exchanged as he gently put her down.

Only after this did I see that while Omar was kneeling to unstick Roxana he must have put his knee squarely into a pile of bird droppings. I tried to remember if we had done any good full-length portraits of him yet. We certainly wouldn't be taking any more now.

In the spirit of trying to make the best of things, I had them walk hand in hand down the pier. Very slowly, avoiding cracks in the boards and bird messes. It was obvious that nothing much of a spontaneous nature would be happening here, but at least we did get some pictures of them walking together and stopping to kiss with a ferry passing silently behind them. I was pleased—and relieved. We had salvaged something from all this.

As we trooped back to the car, Roxana's cell phone rang. Exactly where she had it concealed in that dress of hers I had no idea, but she dug around in the ample folds of satin and came out with her phone. The family members had all arrived at the site and were ready for pictures. We were to hurry back immediately. This solved the question of driving around the city taking pictures, and Roxana looked relieved. We carefully slid Roxana and her dress into the backseat, and Sarah and I crammed ourselves into the front.

"Let's move. It's so hot in here," moaned Roxana. The

driver was being cute and honking the horn for the benefit of passersby.

"Just start the darn car, buddy," said Sarah.

With one last toot of the horn, the driver finally turned the key in the ignition. The engine made no sound. The driver tried again. Nothing. "These old beauties can be a bit temperamental," he said "Nothing to worry about." He looked worried.

"Why don't we get out while he fixes it." Omar's voice was muffled by Roxana's dress.

We spilled out of the car to cheers from the crowd that had gathered to watch. "Can I take a picture of you?" a woman asked Roxana. "Could you walk out on the pier so we have the bridge in the background, or maybe just one by the car?"

I put Sarah in charge of running interference between the sweating bride and the gathering crowd and went to see how Omar was doing. He had persuaded the driver to give him a try at starting the car. Strange noises were coming from under the hood. Then, miraculously, the engine turned over and started to hum. Omar emerged from the driver's seat to a round of applause from the crowd, and we all crammed ourselves into the car as quickly as possible. "Here we go," shouted the driver. The crowd cheered as the car rolled away from the curb. The relief made us all instantly much happier.

We drove about fifteen feet before the car died. The audience groaned. We got out. I suggested a taxi back to the hotel. "Do you know how dirty those are?" said Roxana.

"I can't go in a taxi wearing this dress." Omar looked around rather desperately for a replacement Bentley. "Call the hotel," I suggested. "Someone from your family can come and pick you up." Roxana pulled her cell phone back out from somewhere in her dress and started dialing. But, for the first time all day, she got no answer. Not on her uncle's phone. Not on her mother's phone. Not on the cell phones of any one of the five cousins she tried.

"Wow, what are the chances of that?" Omar wondered.

"We'll walk," said Roxana.

And that's what we did. With a bride wearing five-inch stilettos and a billowing gown, and a disheveled groom in a tuxedo with knees white with seagull dung, and two sweating photographers trying to shoulder camera bags and walk backward in front of the couple to document this procession, we walked fifteen blocks. It turned into quite a party. Horns honked. A tour bus stopped to watch. Passersby shouted out their congratulations.

Roxana and Omar loved it. Roxana stopped worrying about her dress and had a ball. They stopped at the intersections to wave to the crowd, improvised a few dance steps in the middle of the street, and kissed for every camera. They both thought it was hilarious when Omar stepped on a wad of old chewing gum and mugged for my camera as he leaned nonchalantly on a fire hydrant to scrape the gum off his shoe with a stick.

"Get some pictures of us crossing the street," said Roxana. "Did you get a shot of the people on the tour bus watching us?"

"Persians may be crazy," said Sarah, "but I like their style."

As we came around the last corner, Omar swung Roxana into a dip and kissed her. A huge cheer went up from the 140 or so relatives gathered on the steps of the bank.

"Let's go, Claire," said Omar as he put Roxana back on her feet, "we better make this quick. You've got fifteen minutes till showtime."

10

Forward Motion

For a long time after my mother's death I couldn't move. But, as still as you try to stand, as shallowly as you try to breathe, events have a way of shoving you along. I woke up eventually and put my sadness away somewhere private and took a look at what was going to happen next. I knew that things would be different now. I would not go back to New York. Instead, I moved with my mother's old dog, Stalker, into a huge, empty factory space in a nearby town. It had plenty of room for me to build a darkroom and studio. By a stroke of good fortune, the upstairs floor of the building was occupied by a painter whose friendship and appetite for life helped revive my own enjoyment of things. It was clear to me that I could not go back to shooting weddings. It was time now to start doing the work I really wanted to do. I looked for, and found, some good editorial assignments and began advertising for more portrait work—something I had always enjoyed. Through the confidence of an art director willing to take a risk on my relative inexperience, I started working for a new client, a national organization dedicated to setting up mentoring partnerships for at-risk children. Working for these people was sheer joy. So when, having been hired to shoot their annual report, I found myself waiting at the Philadelphia airport to meet the writer who was to travel with me on assignment, I felt I had a plan for the future, and it had nothing to do with wedding photography. It had everything to do with freedom, movement, and work that satisfied both my love of photography and my sense that your work should somehow be in the service of a greater good. I wanted no complications. Then the writer arrived, and we fell in love on the plane. His name was John, and he was newly married. This was complicated. I had never thought about any sort of a long-term relationship for myself. My parents had divorced when I was in my early teens, a fact that was a relief to all of us at the time. But I don't think that the lack of success in my parents' marriage was what had made me disinclined toward commitment. I just didn't see it as relevant in my life. I was busy. At fifteen, I had read Simone de Beauvoir. I admired self-sufficiency. I read Colette and accounts written by early female explorers. I imagined I would travel, work, and take wonderful lovers along the way, lovers who would not interfere with my life. When, considerably older, I left my bruised heart in New York and did go traveling, it was to try to forget my failure at self-sufficiency and to forgive myself for having been so foolish as to get hurt. And when I sent a postcard from India to my onetime love telling him in detail how I had forgotten all about him, I didn't see the humor of it until a lot later.

I did get over it, though, and at some point all the drama

of my broken heart began to look mundane even to me. Too much that really hurt had happened. Too much real loss. My foray into the indulgence of self-mortification felt like a squandering of time, and life was too valuable for any more waste. Even love began to feel like a possibility again—but love with nice, funny, interesting men who wouldn't expect me to stick around very long. I was once more a believer, but one who felt pretty sure about how to protect her heart.

So much for that. I got bowled over. I was going to try to avoid telling you some nonsense about love at first sight, but that's how it went. Right across a crowded airport. He walked up, told me he was the writer assigned to travel with me to work on the annual report I was shooting, and sat down next to me. I looked down at the page of the notebook I was writing in. I wrote the word "trouble" and shut my notebook. I was going to be sensible. And I was. Right up until the moment he folded up his jacket and slipped it under my head as I tried to catch a little sleep on the plane. Right up until I woke up and we started talking. Neither of us seemed to be breathing quite normally. What can I say? That's how it happened. Love like a slap in the face. With a man who was three months married.

I got into my hotel room and shut the door. Absolutely not, I told myself. This was ridiculous. Though my morals might be seriously sketchy by some people's standards, this was not on my list of acceptable behavior. He was married, and I would keep whatever I was feeling to myself. I knew he was feeling the same way I was, and I knew he would do the same thing. We'd both just ignore the whole situation.

The trip felt endless, and far too short. It's hard work maneuvering your way around the obvious. We talked about music, books, history, travel, our lives and passions—the things you talk about at first, wildly happy to discover in another person a mind that challenges and meshes with your own. If you are very lucky, you go on talking that way for years. We talked about everything except what both of us were thinking. Not so much as a word or a touch of any kind to give away anything about what we were both feeling. When we parted at the airport, we shook hands. I was off to Chicago for the next leg of my assignment, and he was headed home.

Sitting on the plane, I thought that I had it all figured out. I should be happy. I now knew that the sort of love I had once feared might not be possible did in fact exist. I had felt it, and I told myself that it didn't matter if I never saw him again because it was enough just to know that it was possible. I told myself lies right through that flight and for a week in Chicago. By the time I made it home I almost believed them.

John had not told himself any lies. He had flown home and told his wife that they could no longer be together.

11

Reverend Doogan

Oh, no, they've hired Doogan," I said. Sarah and I were sitting outside at our favorite coffee shop and going over the list of the next month's weddings.

"Big Doogan? Who's hired him?"

"These guys with the wedding next week."

"That's too bad. They seemed so nice."

"I should warn them. Come on, Sarah, I should, right? Seriously, don't just sit there grinning. I should at least give them a hint. What would you do?"

"I'd sit back and watch the fun."

I used to think that a bride and groom always met in person with the celebrant who would be performing their wedding ceremony—or, at the very least, would have had a telephone conversation with him or her. As it turns out, in this age of e-mail, many people find and book online the person who is to be their officiant. Sometimes they don't actually speak to that person until their wedding day. This might explain Reverend Doogan's booming wedding business. The Reverend is a large man. Extra-large soda and several sides of french fries big. And he's not tall. He always wears a black suit. Always the same black suit. I know it's the same one because the stains are in exactly the same places every time I see him. The suit has a comfortably lived-in look, the black having turned a dusty shade of gray. Reverend Doogan has trouble keeping his white shirt tucked into the front of his trousers. His generous stomach hangs over his straining waistband, bobbing gently when he walks. He has a thatch of unruly white hair, and his eyes have a disconcertingly manic twinkle. Between the jiggling tummy and the twinkling eyes, he could probably earn a little extra cash at Christmas working at Santa Land, if the store owner wasn't too picky. But it's the Reverend's voice that is his crowning glory. A great booming basso profundo, infused with merry little ho-ho-hos. His chuckle is his specialty. Every three sentences or so, he twinkles, chuckles, and exudes warmth. No matter what the circumstances.

I use the term "Reverend" lightly. Exactly how and where he may have been ordained is a mystery. He calls himself a Man of God. His business card reads REVEREND DOOGAN, MAN OF GOD. SUITABLE FOR WEDDINGS, FUNERALS, AND EVENTS. He drives around in a van that he has converted to look like a covered wagon. Window boxes nailed to the sides are filled with plastic flowers. Hand-lettered wooden signs decorate the outside. I'M ON GOD'S BUSINESS. HONK IF YOU LOVE WEDDINGS. REVEREND ON BOARD. WEDDINGS 5 CENTS. I BRAKE FOR BRIDES.

A Reverend Doogan wedding always begins with a

bang. He stands silently for a moment with bowed head, raises his eyes to heaven, looks at his audience, and booms, "Deeeeeerly beeeeeeeeelooved." By drawing out the vowels, he makes these two words last an unbearably long time. All the while, his arms spread wide, he is nodding, smiling, and scanning the crowd with his merry twinkling eyes. At this point, I usually hear a few giggles from the guests. "Folks, let's talk about the holy institution of marriage," says Reverend Doogan, slapping his meaty palms together. He's warming up now, and what better audience than a captive one.

Five minutes later, I see the first signs of panic in the bride and groom. There are small, restless movements. They catch each other's eye. They are realizing that the Reverend is not going to stick to the agreed-upon script. What was listed on the program as a short homily on the meaning of marriage will in fact be a twenty-minute performance by this maniac. At one wedding, I watched a brave groom tap on the Reverend's arm and point to his watch in the middle of one of these monologues. Not in the least put off, Reverend Doogan warmly clapped the groom on the shoulder and boomed out, "Hold on, son, ho-ho-ho. You'll get to kiss her soon enough." Then he picked up right where he had left off.

I have a favorite of all the Reverend's weddings that I've photographed. A Doogan masterpiece. This particular wedding happened about a year ago. I had been contacted by a wonderful couple. Just the sort of people I'm happiest to have come through the door. They seemed blessedly normal and were thrilled to be getting married. Also, they loved my work. This always endears people to me.

"We're not having anyone there but you, so can you be our witness?" asked Elissa, the bride.

"Absolutely, I'd be happy to."

"We're having the ceremony out at the high cliffs near Bodega Bay. We just want to stand alone with the minister and say our vows and then maybe do a few pictures on the beach afterward. Really simple. Do you think that will work?"

Were they kidding? That was my idea of the perfect wedding. "It will be fantastic," I told them. "I can't wait."

I knew that area well, and I loved photographing on those wonderfully craggy, sometimes bleak cliffs along the Northern California coast. Elissa planned to wear a pale pink wedding gown, and Sean, her groom, would be in a tuxedo. I looked forward to photographing them alone on the deserted beach. With luck there would be just a little wind to make things move, and perhaps some fog rolling in.

"Do exactly as you please," said Sean. "We trust you completely. We just want a few nice pictures from our wedding, and we'll be totally happy."

"The main thing to us," added Elissa, "is that there should be no fuss."

I live for clients like these.

*E*lissa and Sean looked excited but cold when I met them at the wedding site on a piercingly windy day. Goose bumps covered Elissa's arms. The groom was a little better off in his tuxedo but still looked mighty cold. They were both in high spirits, though. At the last minute, Elissa's parents had decided to come along. Elissa's mother stood shivering in a pink suit, with a double string of pearls around her neck. The carefully arranged wave of her hair was getting blown about, and she seemed to be having some trouble balancing on the rocky path in her lime green pumps. Elissa's father had green suspenders, to match his wife's shoes, and a jaunty pale pink bow tie. Clearly, this was not the sort of wedding they were used to. They looked frozen but gracious and seemed determined to put a good face on this unorthodox ceremony. We all planned to go down some steps to the beach afterward. There we would be relatively sheltered from the wind by some large rocks and would be able to take some pictures by the ocean.

The five of us stood waiting. Reverend Doogan was late, and I was feeling hopeful. Perhaps the Reverend would hold back just a little since it was so small a group. I liked these people. I admired their determination to be married without ostentation and crazy expense. They had deliberately chosen a quiet, peaceful site. Little did they know they had hired a one-man circus. It was too late now. I kept my mouth shut and my fingers crossed. These people deserved better than to have the ridiculous Reverend come and muck everything up with his theatrics. Maybe he would restrain himself for once. I was working hard on my optimism.

A few minutes later, we all heard the Reverend heading our way.

"Not to worry, not to worry. The Reverend is in the building. Fear not, for I have arrived."

My heart sank. It seemed the Reverend would be playing to a full house, no matter the actual size of the crowd.

"All right, everybody," boomed the Reverend, "follow me." We assembled on a sandy patch of ground near the edge of the cliff.

"Madam," said Reverend Doogan, taking Elissa's mother by the arm, "you stand over here. "Now, no crying yet, you hear?" He gave her a sympathetic little pat.

"Mr. Groom, right next to me, please. Can't risk having him run away, can we?" He winked at Elissa's mother, who looked taken aback. She looked at her daughter and raised her eyebrows expressively. This was not how any of her friends' daughters had been married.

"Now, Dad," continued the Reverend, "here's what I want you to do. And I know it is difficult, sir, believe me, but it is time to give your little girl away to her new care-taker. Every little bird must leave the nest someday and fly free, and today is your birdie's turn to fly. Your job now, Dad, is to take her arm here and walk her in and hand her over to that good man over there."

Elissa's father looked like he was far more likely to be a flight risk than the groom. Both father and daughter plainly hated the idea that Elissa was to be symbolically passed from the care of one man to another. But such was the force of the Reverend's insistence that that was exactly what they did. Everyone was suddenly a bit player in the Reverend's show. Looking acutely uncomfortable, Elissa's father walked his daughter along the rocky path to where Sean stood and placed his daughter's hand into that of his future son-in-law.

Reverend Doogan's eyes twinkled with understanding. He put a sympathetic arm around the father's shoulder and said, "Don't worry, Dad. She'll always be your little girl."

The bride, thirty-eight years old, had plainly not been her father's little girl for quite some time.

"Get a shot of this," said the Reverend to me. I could hear Elissa's mother's teeth chattering. I had some hope that the Reverend would take the hint and keep things simple. Perhaps he would even get cold himself and want to speed things up a bit. But the Reverend was well padded. Speaking to an audience apparently spread far and wide across the clifftop, he intoned, "Welcome, all you good souls who have gathered here today to watch the joining in holy matrimony of these two people."

Several surprised seagulls took flight.

Virtually alone on the windy, barren cliff, the Reverend proceeded to address his audience of hundreds. He spoke, laughed, twinkled, and roared out his approval of the married state. He invited anyone who had any objections to speak them. He quoted Kahlil Gibran, lyrics from "Love Me Tender," and a short except from *Winnie-the-Pooh*. When he began, "How do I love thee, let me count the ways," Elissa's father went to sit on a nearby rock with his head in his hands. Reverend Doogan did everything but a soliloquy from *Hamlet* and a medley of show tunes. He had a wonderful time. The seagulls had settled back in and seemed to appreciate the show. We were frozen.

"Well, my dears," he finally said, "it's time for those rings. But first allow me just to say—"

"Oh good God," burst out Elissa's mother, "haven't you said enough?"

Reverend Doogan looked her up and down. "Madam," he said with great dignity, "as you seem to be in a hurry, we shall proceed."

There was some difficulty getting the rings on due to the shaking of Elissa's frozen hands. The Reverend offered to assist, but Sean said he preferred to do it himself, if the Reverend didn't mind. When at last the couple kissed, Reverend Doogan offered Elissa's mother a handkerchief to dry her tears. She was not crying.

"Would you like me to join you for the family pictures on the beach?" offered the Reverend. Elissa's no was so emphatic that even Reverend Doogan noticed. "I suppose they are anxious to be alone?" He looked a little hurt.

"Everyone's just a bit chilly, Reverend," I said. "I think Elissa's parents need a little time to warm up in the car. I'm sure you don't have time to wait, do you?" I propelled the Reverend firmly toward his truck as I watched Elissa's parents practically running to their car. Elissa and Sean were wrapped up together in Sean's jacket and heading down to the beach.

"Farewell," shouted the Reverend. "Don't you love weddings?" he asked me as we walked along. "I'm off to Napa for another wedding right now. I can't get enough of them. Here are some business cards for you to distribute, and I'd be happy to share with you some lovely testimonials from couples I have joined in marriage. Spread the word. No one does weddings quite like me."

Amen.

12

Rover as Ring Bearer

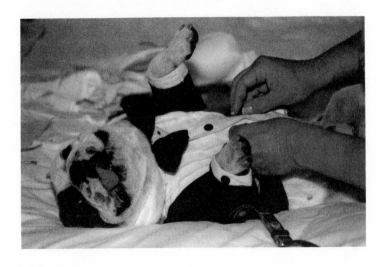

$\mathcal{I}$ usually get up early. I like it. At 5:00 A.M. the house is still. No one is asking for breakfast yet, not even the guinea pigs. Even the family of pigeons that has taken up residence in the old fan vent over the stove haven't started their all-day cooing extravaganza. On these mornings I make my coffee, take a look out the window, and, if I'm feeling productive, sometimes decide to get a little e-mail taken care of before the business of the day begins. Some days that's a really bad idea. Some days I find things like this.

Hi, Claire,

Well, it's only nine months till our big day so of course we're in the middle of lots of wedding planning craziness!! We have a BIG question for you and we'd really appreciate it if you'd get back to us ASAP on this one. You'll see why! We are having a MAJOR PROBLEM. We want to use an ivory tablecloth on our cake table! I know what you're thinking, but don't worry, the cake is not white so we won't have a situation with the colors clashing! But here's the real problem. People are telling me that ivory doesn't photograph well!!? We're pretty upset about it because it took us a super long time to make our linen decisions and it wasn't easy, and now it looks like maybe we'll have to start all over again. Can you please write back to us as soon as possible and let us know if you feel ivory would be a disaster? I also have a major question about nail polish colors, but I'll wait on asking about that so you can just concentrate on the linen question right now. Hope to hear back from you soon!

    Bye,

    Lindsey

I took my coffee and went to read the *Times* on the couch. Sure enough, there it was. News of the world. Evidence of all sorts of things going on out there. Things worth getting worried about, or indignant, or angry. Things that needed attention ASAP like global warming, military aggression, and nuclear proliferation. Not a word about the global implications of Lindsey's table linens. I decided it was best, given my frame of mind, if I wrote back to Lindsey a bit later in the day. In the meantime, I'd give Sarah a call.

I'd forgotten that she doesn't get up quite as early as I do. Actually, she doesn't get up early at all.

"Whaaaat? Whoisis? Why are you calling me?" I heard some sort of snuffling and huffing and then a loud bang. Sarah had dropped the phone. I'm not usually a coward, but this was Sarah. I was just hanging up the phone when she came back on the line. "Don't even think about hanging up, Claire. I know it's you. You better have a good reason for calling me."

"I got an e-mail that made me mad," I said sheepishly.

There was a long silence on the other end of the line. "You got an e-mail that made you mad?"

"I, ah, got a stupid e-mail and I thought I'd, um, tell you about it."

"You thought you'd tell me about it?"

"Did you get a parrot?" Uh-oh, that just slipped out.

There was another long silence. "You got a stupid e-mail and called me at six thirty in the morning and now you're making parrot jokes?"

"Bad idea?"

"Bad idea."

"Want to meet for coffee? A bit later, I mean."

"Nine. And it better be a good e-mail. No, wait, ten. And you're buying." The line went dead.

By ten, Sarah's mood had improved. After apologizing and buying her a double-shot extra-large killer cup of coffee, I showed her the e-mail.

"This crap still gets to you?" was her comment. "Don't you know they love it?"

"Love what?"

"Stress, worrying about this stuff and getting themselves all tied up in knots about the details. They must, or otherwise they wouldn't plan the stuff they do. This is their idea of a good time."

"Oh, come on, Sarah, nobody loves stress."

Sarah sighed. Sometimes I fear that the job of setting me straight on everything will get to be too much for her. "Claire," she began.

I know that tone of voice. It means *Listen up and I'll explain it all to you*. These explanations last a while. "Hang on. I'll just get a refill if it's going to be one of those," I told her.

She handed me her cup. "Same again." Two double-shot coffees; this was Sarah on high octane.

I came back with our cups and settled in to listen. "OK, shoot."

But this was not going to be one of Sarah's long explanations. In fact, all she said was, "Bridget and Walter." She smiled. She had proven her point.

*I*f ever anyone went deliberately in search of worry and massive stress, it was Bridget and Walter. On the checklist of what not to do for a stress-free wedding, they scored a hundred.

The coordinator for Bridget and Walter's wedding called me the week before their ceremony date. "This couple has a death wish." That sounded cheery.

"What's up?" I asked.

"Everything that I tell them is a really bad idea, they go for. And then, as soon as they decide to do something they start worrying about it. I've warned them about the butterfly thing, the dog thing, and the Happy Endings cake thing. They're doing it all."

"Not all of those. Seriously?"

"It's not the sort of thing I joke about," she said gloomily.

"These two are just looking for reasons to worry. And now that it's all set, she keeps calling me to ask if I'm sure it will be OK. And you know what, it's not OK. It is seriously not going to be OK."

"It's her decision, though, right?" I said.

The coordinator gave an unhappy laugh. "Since when doesn't the planner get blamed for the couple's bad decisions?"

She had a point. Still, things did look like they might be interesting from a photography perspective. Even Sarah got quite excited when I told her what was up.

"Train wreck," she said succinctly as we looked over Bridget's ten-page plan for exactly how the day was supposed to go. The schedule was separated into fifteen-minute intervals. "Total train wreck."

*I*t started off quite normally. Normal in terms of an obsessive-compulsive control freak bride, that is. Sarah and I were right on time as we walked into Bridget's suite at the resort where she and Walter were having their wedding. The seven bridesmaids were arguing about something when we arrived. I didn't see Bridget, but a toxic cloud of hairspray was drifting in from the other room of the suite. I sent Sarah in there to say hello and got busy taking the plastic cover off the wedding dress so that I could pose it for the usual dress still-life shot. If you've spent a fortune on your dress, you like to have it photographed hanging prettily on a satin hanger in a picturesque spot with your shoes posed at the hem. I barely had the cover unzipped when a frantic screech came from the bedroom.

"Have you washed your hands?"

I jumped. Was that directed at me? All seven bridesmaids had stopped arguing and were looking at me accusingly.

Bridget came tearing out of the other room. "Don't touch it." Her hair was half done, and she was clutching a giant bottle of water. "No one touches the dress without washing their hands. Please wash your hands if you are going to go near the dress. It's got to stay perfect. You guys"—this last was directed to the bridesmaids—"I'm holding you responsible, is that clear?"

The bridesmaids nodded.

"Claire," Bridget turned back to me, "you understand about the hands, right?" She took an enormous slug of water from the bottle she was holding. "God, I've got to stop hydrating now, I'm supposed to be peeing. I've timed it out. I'll hydrate till a certain time before the ceremony, and then I pee, and then put my dress on. See? That way I'll have enough hydration but won't need to pee until after the ceremony. I've run through it the last couple of days for timing. Ladies," she said to the bridesmaids, "get your dresses on. You have ten minutes. I want you to be completely ready when you fake helping me put my dress on for the pictures. And don't forget to wash your hands." She went back next door.

The room was quiet for a moment, and then all seven bridesmaids started frantically pulling on their dresses.

Sarah came out of the other room. Her eyes looked red. That hair spray can be tough. "I need to use the bathroom," she said.

"Wash your hands," said at least five of the bridesmaids.

Sarah looked outraged. She opened her mouth to answer, but I managed to push her into the bathroom before she could tell them all where to go.

Ten minutes later, we managed, without too much drama, to get Bridget into her dress. Having stood her on a pristine white sheet, we set up three small stools around her and covered her head with a silk scarf to preserve her hairdo and keep makeup off her dress. Three specially chosen bridesmaids lowered the frothy mass of her dress over her head. Bridget shouted muffled directions from inside.

"Is everyone watching, Claire? They should be standing and looking at me. You should get pictures of that." Her head emerged, and someone took off the scarf. "Do we need to do it over?" asked Bridget. "Did they look like they were really watching?"

"They loved it," said Sarah. "They were having the time of their lives. In fact, I've never seen anyone having that much fun. I wish I could have that much—"

I sent Sarah to find the groom.

Bridget looked worried.

"Everything OK?" I asked.

"No," said Bridget. "I have to pee."

Walter was worried, too. The bright blue sky looked suspicious to him. There was possible cloud cover moving in. Of course, if clouds didn't come, the guests might be too hot. He and Bridget had this covered, though. There were dozens of bright Chinese parasols for excessive sun and a pile of striped blue golf umbrellas for possible rain. In fact, the day was bright, warm, and about as perfect as any couple could wish for on their wedding day. The grass in the field where the wedding was taking place was a brilliant shade of green. A path of yellow rose petals led to the spot where the ceremony would happen.

"She wanted them strewn symmetrically," said the coordinator, sounding a little tired. "She also called me at seven this morning to tell me she was concerned. She had a nightmare last night that when she made it to the altar and turned around there were flower arrangements from the previous event mixed in with hers. She told me that she didn't want to see a single flower that was left over from the ceremony before hers or she didn't know what she'd do. She just called Walter on his cell to go check the site and make sure. Oh my God." She turned pale. "The guests are walking on the petals. Bridget will kill me. No guests are permitted to mess up the petals, was what she told me. Please no! Ma'am, sir. Go around, go around!" She dashed away, waving frantically at the bemused guests. Bridget and Walter's worry was contagious.

Half an hour later, the aisle was still perfect, the sun was still shining with just the correct level of brightness, and the guests had all found their seats. Walter was in place and waiting for his bride. He looked excited but worried. All the bridesmaids made it down the aisle. Their seven shades of green dresses exactly matched the seven shades of green in the groomsmen's ties. As directed, they had arranged themselves by height, and the color shadings of the men's ties and women's dresses were symmetrical on either side of Walter. Bridget would be pleased.

Then Sarah grabbed my arm. "Disaster one." She pointed to the back of the aisle. "Here we go."

Bridget and Walter had invited their beagle, Bubba, to the wedding. Worse, they had given him an important and exciting job. Bubba was the flower girl. With a little push on his rump from the coordinator, he started down the aisle. He made it halfway and stopped to have a long pee on a chair leg.

The coordinator shrugged. "Damn. What can you do? We hydrated that dog, then walked him just when Bridget said to."

The guest seated nearest Bubba's stream moved so quickly to avoid getting soaked that he knocked over his own chair and that of the woman sitting next to him. Oblivious to the havoc in his wake, Bubba started off again, only to stop and sit down a moment later. It seemed he had just fully registered the elaborate wreath of ivy, daisies, and orange blossom that some poor put-upon florist had spent hours weaving for his furry head—no doubt exactly to Bridget and Walter's specifications. Bubba settled in for a good scratch.

Bridget's ceremony was coming apart just like that wreath. The guests were laughing. Everyone, including Walter, was looking at Bubba and not at Bridget, who was stuck at the end of the aisle being upstaged by a beagle now wearing a mangled wreath around his neck.

"I like that dog," said Sarah thoughtfully.

Walter decided to take charge. He started down the aisle to get Bubba. For some reason, the musicians thought that this was the cue to start the bride's processional music, so Bubba was frog-marched the rest of the way down the aisle to the strains of the Trumpet Voluntary while the co-ordinator frantically signaled to the musicians to stop play-ing. At last, with Bubba's collar held firmly by Walter's mother in the front row, and Walter back in position, the musicians began again. This time Bridget made it to the al-tar. But Bubba wasn't quite finished yet. As soon as he saw his beloved Bridget and Walter standing just a few feet away from him and realized that he couldn't get to them, he did what all good beagles do: He howled. And he kept howling, until finally he had to be dragged away, still howling, which reduced the tiny ring bearer to tears.

"Don't hurt the doggie," he wailed miserably. He was led away howling, too.

When the sounds of lamentation, both human and dog, had died away in the distance, Walter and Bridget got mar-ried.

At this point you might almost think that Bridget and Walter were home free, but Sarah and I knew better. The ceremony ended, and the bride and groom kissed. It was hard to get a good shot of the kiss since Bridget wouldn't let Walter's lips actually touch hers because of her lipstick, but I did my best.

Just then, we saw the coordinator waving her arms up and down. It was time for disaster number two. "Here we go," said Sarah grimly.

"Save as many of them as you can," I said. I didn't like this part.

Bridget and Walter had decided to have a butterfly re-lease. Here's how it's supposed to go. You kiss and turn from the altar into a cloud of colorful butterflies released by your guests. You walk down the aisle through this magical cloud and wander away into the distance, leaving your guests to marvel at the butterflies as they fly happily away. In your dreams, as Sarah would say. Here's how it really goes, and how it went for Bridget and Walter. They kissed and turned to come back down the aisle. Right on cue, their guests each opened the little flat white box they had been given at the start of the ceremony. Boxes that had been delivered three days before and had been sitting somewhere in the typically chilly Northern California weather. One hundred and twenty butterflies staggered out, stunned by the light, and flopped down onto the flower petals, or just fell out helplessly into the guests' laps. All the kids went crazy. Some started to cry because they thought the butterflies were dead; others immediately rushed to follow the strange and horrible instincts of certain small children and started dismembering a few. This made the crying children start screaming and a few of the parents start yelling.

And there stood Walter and his bride, faced with several no-win options. Should they proceed down the aisle and trample butterflies to the tune of the cries of distressed children, or slink off around the side so as to avoid both the horrified stares of their guests and a potential massacre? Now Bridget really had something to worry about, and she was not handling it well. In fact, she froze. Then she broke and ran, with Walter right behind her, around the outside of the chairs and off toward the distant tent.

"The bride and groom will now have a few moments to themselves and join you all shortly," announced the coordinator calmly. She'd seen it before. "Everybody please proceed to the patio area for cocktails and leave the butterflies where they are."

The guests moved away to get their drinks. Only one little boy stayed behind with his mother. He stood for a moment holding his mother's hand and looking down at a pile of several tangled butterflies. Finally, he said, "Mommy, what happens to the butterflies now?" Which was exactly what Sarah and I were wondering, too. But we had work to do, and the day was far from over.

When it comes to wedding stress, one of the definite high points can be the bustling of the dress. It doesn't have to be. You can choose a dress without a train, and then you don't have to bustle at all. Or a simple one-button bustle that takes two minutes and one helpful friend to sort out. Bridget, naturally, had gone for the worst-case scenario. Her bustling system was the sort that requires a tutorial. Three bridesmaids, carefully chosen for their manual dexterity, had gone to the dressmaker's with Bridget to get their bustling lesson. Now, their powers of memory were being put severely to the test.

Bridget's dress was supposed to have twelve color-coded strings with tiny matching colored loops to tie them to, and some of the strings had gone missing. All three bridesmaids were up under Bridget's dress when Sarah and I found them in the ladies' room. One bridesmaid was guarding the door and telling guests who needed the bathroom they'd have to wait.

"I knew this would go wrong," said Bridget. "I warned you guys to study your notes from the lesson. You knew you'd have to help me with this. I can't believe you can't figure out a simple little bustling assignment."

For twenty minutes they fumbled around under there, as Bridget got more and more upset. Many of the loops seemed to be buried in places Bridget's friends didn't want to go. To add insult to injury, Bridget had worn no underwear under her gown for fear of showing panty lines. The demands of friendship were severe.

"Does anyone have a flashlight?" gasped a flushed bridesmaid crawling out from under Bridget's dress. For some odd reason, Sarah had one in her camera bag. Big bonus points for us. Bridget gave us an approving look, and the bridesmaid vanished with Sarah's flashlight. That did the trick, and five minutes later, Bridget's helpers staggered away to the bar. Bridget had now missed her entire cocktail hour.

"I knew this would happen," she said, and went to find Walter.

"She looked sort of happy about it." I was confused. "Why?"

"It vindicates her," said Sarah. "Now she can tell all her friends that she was right to worry. Hey, they took my flashlight. I knew that would happen."

Apart from the fact that Bridget and Walter had, against their wedding planner's and caterer's advice, chosen a menu that required their guests to sit still for a two-hour, five-course formal meal, things went smoothly for a while. The guests were bored and the food not very good (it's hard to cook elaborate meals in a tent kitchen), but Bridget and

Walter looked happy as they walked around the tent making sure that each course was presented correctly and complaining to the kitchen when it was not. Apart from having to keep the chef from strangling them both, even the planner seemed to think the worst was over. Until Happy Endings arrived for the cake setup.

Happy Endings is notorious. Its people are creative and, unless you like to worry, creative is not a good thing at your wedding. Reliable, recommended, experienced, these are good things. Creative, cutting-edge, and experimental, these spell trouble. The Happy Endings designers like to try something new. Something that will surprise and impress your guests. Or else they're a bunch of sadists who get their kicks out of messing with brides' minds. I'm not sure. For Bridget and Walter they had come up with a grand idea. They were decorating the wedding cake with fruit. Whole, big, heavy fruit. All seven tiers of the cake were being festooned with whole lemons, apples, and pears.

"Think they'll put a nice banana on the top?" I asked Sarah. We were watching the decorating team at work.

"Grapefruit," she giggled. "No, watermelon."

We were laughing too hard now, and the designers gave us a dirty look, so we took a few pictures and wandered away. The Happy Endings people never actually stick around to watch the happy endings of their cakes. They design and go, after giving me their business card and telling me to be sure to send them some pictures.

The ending for Bridget and Walter's cake was one of the best I've ever seen. The cake table was set up at the edge of the dance floor. The idea was that Walter and Bridget would do their first dance, and then Bridget would dance with her father and afterward move straight to the cake table to meet Walter and cut their cake with the assembled guests watching. Bridget had planned it very carefully. By this time we'd all been in the tent a long while. The plastic side flaps were down because Walter worried about wind, and the heat from the cooking tent and all the bodies had made things very hot. The cake had been sitting, fully decorated, for two hours. The timing was perfect. The first lemon hit the dance floor right in the middle of the father-daughter dance. Then the icing gave way entirely, and the guests chased the escaped pears and apples around the dance floor to the tune of "What a Wonderful World." Sarah and I got some truly memorable shots. I didn't put those pictures in Bridget's album because, unfortunately, she got a little upset.

"Oh, they loved it," said Sarah. "Those two wouldn't have been happy without the stress. For years they'll have the fun of telling everyone how time-consuming their wedding planning was. It gives them something to think about until they start worrying about buying a house and stressing about having kids and paying for college."

"You think?" I wasn't entirely convinced. Could people really want that kind of stress in their lives?

"Absolutely," said Sarah. One of her feet was bouncing up and down. She was having trouble sitting still. Two double-shot killer coffees will do that to you. It was time to wrap this up, but I still needed to know what I should write back to my tablecloth-challenged client of the morning.

"Easy," said Sarah. "Just tell her that ivory won't work and will look terrible. Then she'll have to start the whole linen planning over again. She'll be in heaven. It'll give her and her fiancé something to worry about. Happiest time of their lives. They'll never have so much in common again. Listen, I gotta go work out or something. This coffee has got me jumpy. Just give 'em what they need."

13

Dash Pierce

$\mathcal{W}$hen I describe Dash Pierce, people don't believe me. I can understand that. It's hard to believe Dash Pierce even when you meet him in person. He's that odd. We met first by telephone.

"Dash here. Uh, Pierce. Dash Pierce, of Pierce and Pierce. Productions. I'm the Dash part. I need someone for three weeks from now. Badly. Can you, I mean if it's really important, be available for that?"

In the wedding business this is unusual. Most people book you with a very long lead time. They're afraid that if they don't lock in their preferred vendors early, they'll miss their chance. This is usually true. But it was the first week of February in San Francisco, the weather was wet and predictably unpredictable, and booking at the last minute at this time of year was not unheard of. It's also a time of year when I am predictably broke, so I said, "Why don't you tell me a bit more about what you're looking for in the way of photography."

Dash sounded excited. "We've got this amazing airplane hangar. Not in use now, of course. Couldn't really do that, could you? I mean, planes coming in and out during the party and all. Wow. That would be so wild, though, huh? So no, we're not messing with that stuff. It will be all sort of green and white and gold, but not some puke green. Chartreuse is what I'm thinking. There's going to be a pale green lounge area with this crazy deep shag carpeting, a real field-of-carpet thing like grass but totally different. Get it? And a white grand piano, a caviar bar, and these fluffy green blankets and pillows on round poufy chartreuse couches. Everything shaggy and poufy. Nice!"

Dash went on for a long time. I think he forgot I was there. His voice kept losing volume and then coming back again. He went on to describe an altar made entirely of purple orchids and a massive banquet table to seat two hundred guests. There would be thousands of pink lights and gold urns dripping with parrot tulips. He said something about Versailles and something about Disneyland. I was having trouble following the conversation because even when Dash turned his personal volume back up, he would keep losing his place in his train of thought. It was as though he was continually being interrupted, but the person interrupting him was himself. It was disconcerting. I tried to bring him back on track.

"You're looking for a wedding photographer, then?"

"We'll have a piano. A white baby grand. Did I say that already? And, uh, yeah, like a loungy sort of, you know, type of feeling. Right?"

"Like a lounge?"

"Yes! Exactly. That's brilliant. And we'll completely light it all, so no worries for you. You'll love it. You'll be the photographer. There will be a lot of green, but I figure you can handle that, right? Hey, you're the pro. The thing is to keep it all moving forward and stuff. You won't believe the ice sculpture thing we're going to have. Make sure you get good shots of that, because, you know, I'll seriously need copies of those. Mercedes wants something really hip and different."

"Mercedes?" I had interrupted him. It took almost a full minute before he spoke again.

"She's the bride. Mercedes." He sounded relieved to have retrieved that piece of information from wherever he had stored it. "So," he said, "we just need someone to show how totally cool it is and that's you."

"You've seen my work, then? I'm just wondering how you found me."

"I, ah, I forget. But I know that a caterer who knows a friend of mine said you were perfect. Or something. So what do you think? Sounds good, right?"

It sounded like a headache, and a job I was totally un-suited for. As far as I could tell, the situation called for someone who did a very different kind of work than I did. They needed a photographer who would bring lots of lights and specialized equipment—and maybe a half dozen assist-ants to set it all up—and would enjoy lighting and photo-graphing interiors in color. Not to mention someone with a license to practice psychotherapy. This was definitely not me. I was intrigued by the odd sound of it all, but in keep-ing with my firm belief that people should get the right person to photograph their wedding and that I should try to avoid walking into messes when I've been given fair warning, I told Dash that I was absolutely not the woman for the job. The more I told him, the more he seemed convinced that I was. I finally ended the conversation by just saying no. I gave him a few names of photographers who might be more suitable. He was still mumbling something when I hung up.

I would've bet a great deal of money that I'd never hear from Dash again. I would have lost. Two days later, Dash called back.

"So, when are you coming to check out the site?" said Dash. "You're gonna love it. This space will totally blow your mind." Something that had apparently already been taken care of in Dash's case. We set up a time to meet. I had to admit, I was pretty curious.

I hadn't really made a mental picture of Dash. Seeing him uncurl his very tall frame from a red Mini Cooper was like watching a contortionist's act. "You can park these anywhere," he said, "but they're small, you know? Like, just really made for little people. Not midgets or anything. I don't have a problem with midgets at all." He looked worried, as though he hadn't quite registered my exact height yet and might have offended me.

"Hi," I said, putting out my hand. "I'm Claire." I thought we might at least try for a semblance of normalcy.

Dash looked at my hand for a moment and then grabbed it and gave it a good shake. "Hey, wow. Claire. So here we are." He now appeared to be at a loss for words and looked at me hopefully, as if wondering what we should do next. He was gaunt, and jittery. Though he was probably only in his thirties, his hair was completely white. His right hand tapped a continual nervous accompaniment on his thigh to a song that only he could hear. His eyes kept flicking to the left and right as we talked. It was hard to stop myself looking off to the side to try to catch a glimpse of whatever Dash was seeing. I guessed Dash had done an awful lot of chemical damage to himself sometime in the not too distant past.

"Shall we go see the space?" I tried.

Dash started. "Let's go," he said. And off we went to explore the cavernous hangar.

Dash jittered and took cell phone calls and tried to explain his vision.

"The groom is a very rich man," said Dash suddenly. "We're talking really, really rich." He looked at me expectantly.

"How nice," I said. I wasn't sure what else to say.

"The point is," said Dash, "It's no holds barred on the budget, and she really wants to impress his friends. She wants things totally unique and stuff. Give them a shock. That's why she hired me. Right? 'Cause I'm totally unique and there's almost no one like me." He thought for a moment. "Maybe no one."

"Why's it so important to impress his friends?" I asked.

Dash panicked. He hadn't realized a question was coming his way. He glanced wildly from side to side, trying to figure out who had asked him what, and why. He looked at me anxiously.

"What do you think?"

I was tempted to say, "I asked you first," just to see what he'd do, but that seemed mean.

"Well, I think that if anyone can do it, you can, Dash." He looked pleased.

"I'm pretty good at most stuff. Did I mention the gold urns with parrot tulips? They won't know what hit them." Dash was on a roll. He looked ecstatic.

"Sounds unique to me," I said.

Dash's vision was a success, if your idea of success is a shock for the senses in an airplane hangar. There were green poufy things to sit on and shag carpets. There was a white piano and an ice sculpture of something I couldn't quite make out. I barely saw the bride, but when I did she looked happy. As soon as he could escape after the ceremony, the groom went outside to smoke cigars for the rest of the evening. The guests mostly just looked cold and uncomfortable. They were painfully polite. Perhaps they were impressed. Dash certainly thought so. He waved me over from the far side of the room, where he had collapsed on one of the couches in a dark corner as soon as he had made it through setup. "They all love it." He looked out blearily at the room. "I better get ready. Everyone's gonna be calling Dash now."

I got a phone call from Dash a few weeks later. He sounded upset. "Claire. I thought you were going to send me a CD with some shots from the wedding? I've got a client meeting like two minutes from now. I need those pictures, Claire."

"Hello, Dash. This is Dash, right? I sent you a CD by FedEx a week ago, just like I promised."

"No way. I never saw anything. Absolutely not, no."

"Hold on. I'll call FedEx and get back to you." So I called. They gave me the name of the person who had signed for the package when it was delivered.

I called Dash back. "Hello, Dash. It was delivered five days ago, and someone named Marina Perez signed for it."

"What! There's no way that can be right. I don't know anyone called Marina Perez, and why the hell would she be at my house signing for my CD?"

"I don't know, Dash, but that's what they told me."

"Wait. Hold on. Someone takes care of my kids. I gotta ask my wife what her name is. The lady who takes care of my kids, I mean. I know my wife's name." He thought for a minute. "Her name is Gwen. But I have no idea what that other lady is called. She's been coming here for years, and I bet she'd sign for a package, right? I'll go see if I can find out her name, and if it's the same name then she should know where the package is, right? I'll call you if it's not her."

I haven't heard from Dash since.

14

Love and Panic

John had ended his marriage. He was judged harshly by some, and I was told that anyone who could do this to one person would most certainly do it to me one day. While I admired his courage in stopping something before the mistakes could multiply and in behaving honorably toward his wife by being honest with her, others saw his actions as selfish, rash, and impulsive. Once married, friends told him, even unhappily or mistakenly so, you should stay put and try to make it work. So went the conventional wisdom. Live with your mistakes, don't try to correct them. I kept my distance and waited while the dust settled. If we were going to start something, it wouldn't happen before the past was dealt with. Though I may have been a catalyst, I had no intention of being anything more until things were squared away.

At the end of the day, even the most wounded party had on some level acknowledged that a mistake had been made, and I had found the companion I needed, a man with an ardent heart. Honest and brave and true was what we decided our partnership would be. And we would never argue about parking tickets or who did the laundry. We were planning a life that was clearly going to have plenty of disagreements, an awful lot of surprises, and absolutely no boredom. It was irresistible.

We loaded my old dog into my extremely old pickup truck and left the East Coast to move to California to start a new life together in a place where I would be less haunted by the material reminders of my mother's death and John could think more clearly about the choices he had made. Along the way we documented my grouchy old dog's progress across the continent. Stalker Dog at Graceland, looking bemused. Stalker Dog locked in the car by mistake on Route 66 and being rescued by a state trooper. Stalker Dog in big-sky country looking fed up with all the pictures. Stalky stuck in snowdrifts, and in the desert learning, painfully, why it's best to keep your distance from a cactus. And mostly, Stalker Dog sitting on the bed in various cheap motels across America eating fast food and looking ready to get wherever the hell it was we were dragging her in her old age. Little did she know we were planning her retirement in paradise.

We set up house in a tiny town a couple of hours north of San Francisco. There were apple orchards and vineyards and redwoods. People wore tie-dye and carried their groceries home in Guatemalan string bags. They made their own goat cheese. After milking their own goats. At the annual apple blossom festival, twenty dachshunds walked in the town parade right behind the women's drumming circle, Green Party representatives, and the association of vegan bakers. One day a group of women celebrated their right to have bare breasts if they wanted by baring their breasts in the town square. At least, I think that was the point. In any case, it was a popular event. On the bulletin board at the local organic grocery store were posters for Wicca meetings, self-actualization sessions, aromatherapy classes, Waldorf schools, and support groups for the wheat intolerant.

Our home was a simple, round, yurt-like building in a grove of eucalyptus trees overlooking a valley. It had sea-grass matting on the floor, one burner to cook on, a refrigerator the size of a microwave, and no furniture. Perfect. Except we were broke. We both needed to start working. John began a new job and I went looking for a way to make a living doing the only thing I wanted, or knew how, to do.

In our schizophrenic town of tie-dye-wearing, SUV-driving, teepee-dwelling, dreadlocked millionaires, there happened to be a cutting-edge technology publishing company. For reasons that were typically cloudy but probably had mostly to do with the fact that we were running out of grocery money every month, John moved from the world of nonprofits, where he had been a writer, and jumped into the sterile vacuum of Internet marketing. The dinner table conversation at our house got far less interesting, but the rent was paid on time.

I didn't do so well. I was anxious not to shoot any more weddings and hopeful that I'd find work as a freelance photographer, but that takes time. There were bills to pay, and

I didn't have the luxury of moving slowly. I needed to do my part to keep our life afloat. I had to find a job fast. On top of everything else, I felt like a fish out of water in this new place. No one wore black or made sarcastic comments. I preferred my coffee with real milk instead of soy. I went to a birthday party where they served birthday bread instead of cake because it was healthier, and nobody there thought that was funny but me. I got chased by a group of wild turkeys when I went out running. No one seemed to see the irony of the giant SUVs with bumper stickers that told me not to trade blood for oil. I could not visualize world peace. I browsed at the local Goddess Shop feeling decidedly un-goddess-like. I was unable to identify even one of my chakras. I read a lot. I even tried soaking in an enzyme mud bath that was supposed to help disperse my negativity but instead gave me a rash. I took long solitary drives along the coast and admired the scenery. I was reminded of all the reasons that landscape photography didn't interest me in the least. I panicked.

Why was I living in a town in the middle of nowhere with someone whose conversation now sounded like a technical manual? Granted, I loved him dearly, but somehow I was getting lost in the shuffle. I felt less brave, less like myself. I was afraid I would never have an original thought again. No more adventures. I stopped photographing altogether. I wore baggy CP Shades outfits and, worst, I got a day job. I was now selling paintings in a Thomas Kinkade gallery. I spent whole days of my life describing Thomas Kinkade as "the painter of light" and selling paintings on the basis of what would match someone's couch.

I had to watch an informational video about how Thomas Kinkade spent Mother's Day with his mother. I had to accept the fact that he was the most widely collected artist in America. Clearly, I had hit bottom. Stress-reducing candles, goddess massage, and solitary beach walks were not going to sort all this out.

15

Brenda's Bridesmaids

$\mathcal{S}$arah was sick. This didn't happen very often, so I was taking it seriously. I had come to see her and had brought presents: the latest *People* magazine, a burrito from her favorite Mexican place, a large double-shot latte, and a bar of chocolate that I had found in the back of the cupboard and must have been left over from Halloween because I never buy candy.

"That was left over from Halloween, wasn't it?" said Sarah. "And who in their right mind brings a burrito to someone with the stomach flu?"

She had a point, but still, it didn't seem very generous of her to be so ungracious.

"I was trying to be nice, you know. Anyway, how'd you know about the candy?" I was sort of impressed she'd figured it out so fast.

Sarah looked at me with what can only be described as pity, lay back down on her pillow, and closed her eyes. "Claire," she said, "look at the candy bar."

There was a picture on the wrapper of Big Bird wearing a Dracula costume. Well, yes, I suppose that might give it away.

"I'll take the coffee and the magazine, though." She sat back up. "Anyway, you can't fool me. The only reason you're here is because you've got Brenda's scary bridesmaids this weekend and you don't want to work alone."

It was true. We had just four days till Brenda and the Bridesmaids, and I really did want Sarah to be there.

"You know you want to be there," I said. Sarah loved weddings that looked like they'd be trouble. And ten brides-maids in open revolt meant trouble.

"Just do me a favor," I said, "and rest up. Do whatever you need to do to get yourself better by Saturday, OK?" I found her some Pepto Bismol to wash down her burrito and left her reading about the latest star to be sent to rehab. I knew she'd eat the candy bar as soon as I left. Sarah hates to admit it but she has a serious sweet tooth. She looked better already. I crossed my fingers for Saturday.

*S*ure enough, Sarah was back in the game by the week-end, but still tired and very testy. I was going to have to tread carefully. We headed out of San Francisco to meet Brenda at Napa's most expensive resort destination. They didn't go quite as far as printing that on their brochures, but they might as well have.

"I don't like this place," said Sarah as we headed up the unmarked private road that led to the resort.

"It's pretty, though. Makes our job easier, right?" This was probably a foolish response on my part. Playing Polly-anna to Sarah's grumpiness never worked.

"You know who stays here?" Sarah continued as though I hadn't said a word. "A bunch of people who want everyone to know they're ridiculously rich. Then they wander around pretending that they're just ordinary people at summer camp staying in their little rustic cabins. Of course, those cabins have flat-screen TVs, private decks with hot tubs, cute guys in uniform who deliver DVDs and champagne, and very quiet Spanish-speaking people who will come in and pick up their wet towels off the bathroom floor where they just drop them because they're spoiled rotten." Sarah paused for breath.

"Would you stay here if they offered you a room?" I asked.

"In a heartbeat," said Sarah.

At the Resort That Must Not Be Named, a general hushed air of self-satisfaction prevailed. When we arrived, my dirty old car was whisked away to someplace where it wouldn't offend anyone's sensibilities, and we were bundled into our private golf cart and zipped to Brenda's suite. Everything sounded quiet as we walked up the path to the four-room cabin that Brenda had booked for herself and her bridesmaids. This was a good sign. There were ten bridesmaids plus Brenda in there, so if they were fighting, we probably would have heard it from outside.

"Ready?" I asked Sarah.

"Ready as I'll ever be," she said.

I knocked on the door.

*I*t wasn't Brenda we were worried about. Granted, she had made some horrible mistakes, and she was bossy and very sure of how she wanted things to be done, but that was nothing unusual. It was her bridesmaids. Combine one bossy bride with ten bridesmaids with serious attitude, shake well, and you've got big trouble. To Brenda's constant frustration, her bridesmaids hadn't read the manual of proper wedding etiquette. They just wouldn't behave the way Brenda wanted. At one point during the past year things had escalated to the point of open mutiny, and Brenda had almost lost half her bridal crew over the issue of dresses, but somehow she had smoothed things over.

Brenda's bridesmaids included her two sisters, the groom's sister, a cousin she had not seen since kindergarten that her mother insisted she ask, and six friends of her own, some of them dating back to elementary school. Now, you can be pretty certain that in a group of ten women you will get a variety of body types. So why Brenda had chosen a strapless, form-fitting sheath of peach silk is hard to imagine. But the fact remains that once you agree to be a bridesmaid, you are just supposed to look at the hideous dress that has been chosen for you and suck it up. Those are the rules, except not for this crew.

Both Brenda's sisters were extremely large. They flat-out refused to wear the dress. The groom's sister called Brenda to tell her that she thought the color clashed with her skin tone and that she was too short for that style. What's more, she was certain that, because of the dress, all the groomsmen would be keeping their fingers crossed that they'd get matched with the tall bridesmaid and not stuck with her. Brenda's oldest friend called to say her bottom was too big for the dress and what the hell was Brenda thinking? Brenda told her there was still time for her to lose weight before the wedding. Tact was not Brenda's strong suit. Another dear friend was six months pregnant. She wrote Brenda a two-page letter accusing her of gross insensitivity and saying that worrying about the dress might induce early labor and that was probably what Brenda wanted. Brenda cried, then called her, and they made up, but things were still pretty rocky. Everyone else was unhappy, too. Their reasons included the fact that the dress cost too much and was the absolute worst possible choice for anyone with a concave chest, arms that jiggled, or a tattoo of her ex-boyfriend's name on her shoulder—didn't Brenda know he'd be at the wedding? How could she be so mean? The tattooed bridesmaid also made a point of reminding Brenda that she didn't believe in shaving, so Brenda had better be OK with hairy legs and armpits. Brenda cried again, and then called me to ask about retouching to remove body hair.

The only bridesmaid who was delighted with the dress was Brenda's cousin. She turned out to be skinny and long-legged and to have 34C breasts. Unfortunately, instead of counting her blessings and keeping her mouth shut, she had the bright idea of e-mailing the other bridesmaids to say she thought they should stop complaining, think of Brenda's needs, and not be so selfish. Plus, she thought the dress was cute. They all hated her, even before they saw what she looked like.

The bridesmaids may have been breaking the rules and giving Brenda a pretty hard time, but they had a point. Each of them knew that every other female guest at the wedding would be wearing some sort of sexy little cocktail dress that was well suited to her body type and that after the bride and groom's first dance the bridesmaids would all be invited out onto the dance floor for the humiliation of dancing in those dresses in front of an audience. And anyone who has ever worn silk can tell you, it shows sweat. Especially the nervous kind of "my dress does not fit and I feel like a conspicuous jerk" sweat. It shows up in large, dark half circles under the arms, and it will leave a shadow-like stain even after you stand for ten minutes with your arms raised in front of the hand dryer in the bathroom.

Several of the bridesmaids began to wonder if this was personal. Perhaps they were remembering what they had made Brenda wear as a bridesmaid at their own weddings, or the boyfriend or favorite pair of shoes that they had borrowed from Brenda and had neglected to return. By now every one of the bridesmaids was wishing desperately that she had never agreed to be in the wedding, and Brenda was wondering if it was too late to just stand up alone with the groom.

Brenda tried to reason with her moaning attendants: "You'll get a ton of use out of those dresses. The style is so classic. You'll definitely be able to wear them again!" She also let them know that, although they would need to buy and dye shoes to go with the dresses, she was going to give them "the really sweet little peach-colored purses" as a gift. That didn't seem to help at all.

Finally, she told them they could have the dresses altered to any style they wanted, and things calmed down for a while.

When Sarah and I walked in, the room was very quiet. There were bridesmaids scattered around the room in various states of undress, but no one was chatting or arguing. In fact, the atmosphere was positively funereal. There was no sign of Brenda.

"Something's up," I said to Sarah.

"Gee, you think?" she answered. I decided to ignore her.

Brenda's two sisters came over, looking grim.

"We need to talk," said one of them, and they led us back outside.

"Some things haven't gone so well," said the sister who was clearly the older of the two. "We're trying to help Brenda with it, so don't say anything when you see her."

"What happened? I mean, is she all right?" I couldn't imagine what on earth could have created this mood of tragedy. Perhaps Brenda had had some sort of dire medical diagnosis, or maybe someone close to her had died.

"It's her face," said the older sister.

"And some other stuff, too," the younger sister added. "You'll see. Come on." We went inside.

By now most of the bridesmaids were in their peach-colored dresses. They all looked fine. Well, they all looked like bridesmaids, which means they were wearing silly clothes that didn't fit very well, but other than that they looked fine. And still no one was complaining. That was the most worrying thing of all.

Brenda's older sister spoke up. "OK, everyone. This is Brenda's day, and you all know she's had some challenges to deal with. Let's do our best to make sure she goes down the aisle feeling like a princess." Everyone nodded solemnly. Clearly, the tragedy was of such a scale as to transform even this group of disgruntled women into textbook bridesmaids.

I was impressed by the way they had risen to the occasion. I didn't say that to Sarah, though. She was in too foul a mood to be impressed by anything, though the way things were going so far did seem to have caught her interest. She was busy getting her camera set up for whenever Brenda would appear.

"It's time to help Brenda put on her dress," said the groom's sister. "Everyone ready? Do you want to go get her?" she asked Brenda's sisters.

They went into the room next door. There was some whispering, and they came back out with Brenda.

"Yikes," said Sarah. "What the hell happened to you?"

I could have killed her.

Actually, though, it was fine. It broke the tension. Especially since the next thing Sarah said was, "Don't worry. I've seen worse. We can fix this."

It's true that both Sarah and I like problems. It's one of the reasons we really do get along so well. Give us a bride in trouble, and we're on it—and poor Brenda was in trouble. She'd made two of the worst mistakes a bride can make the day before her wedding: She'd gone to a spray-on tanning parlor for the first time, and she'd given herself her very first lip wax. She looked like a spotted giraffe with a huge mustache-shaped scab on her upper lip. Not a good look for anyone.

All the bridesmaids chimed in with advice and sympathy. We set up a chair in the middle of the room, and Sarah went off to find the makeup artist Brenda had banished from the suite earlier in the day.

"There's nothing they can do." Brenda was weeping. "I look like an idiot. I'm hideous."

A cry went up from the bridesmaids. "Oh, honey, it'll be fine."

"You'll be so cute."

"We love you."

"You'll look like a total princess."

"No one will even be able to tell, I swear."

Normally the endless chorus of bridesmaids telling the bride how lovely she is makes me nuts. It usually sends Sarah outside for some air after she catches my eye and pretends to be gagging. It often goes on from the time the bride gets her makeup on to seconds before she goes down the aisle. The bridesmaids seem to think it's their job to tell the bride how perfect she is, while she in return gushes on and on about everything from their flawless eyebrows to how she just wishes she were as lovely as they are and how any one of them would look better in her dress than she does. No one means a word of it. It's all straight out of the bridesmaid script. But these women were different. They had given Brenda a hard time for the last six months, and they had plenty of reasons to think that what had happened to Brenda today was pretty funny, and perhaps even fair payback for the dresses they were being forced to wear. Instead, they really did seem to want to help her. They switched smoothly into super-bridesmaid mode and set to work convincing Brenda she was the loveliest bride they'd ever seen.

Sarah came back in with Chloe, the makeup artist. I was relieved to see that Brenda had made a good choice when she hired her makeup person. Chloe is Australian, unflappable, and very good at her job. She'd obviously been filled in on the details of the disaster because she took one look at

Brenda and said, "No worries. Let's get this sorted, shall we? Can someone get me a Diet Coke?" She looked at Brenda again and added, "Make that two."

One of Brenda's sisters headed for the minibar, Chloe rolled up her sleeves, and Brenda began to look slightly less tragic.

Chloe worked on Brenda for two hours. The bridesmaids were magnificent. They brought Brenda drinks and food and gave her continual updates on the wonderful job Chloe was doing. They quietly hid all the mirrors in the room, moving a large potted plant to cover the one on the wall. They massaged her feet and told her that none of the guests would even notice if the wedding started an hour or two late because everyone always expects weddings to start late. They told her how much they had come to love their dresses and even their peachy-colored pumps. They thanked her for their cute little purses and agreed that they'd get lots of use out of them in the future. They told her she was beautiful.

By the time Chloe was finished, she was clearly exhausted, but Brenda's mustache scab was almost hidden by multiple layers of makeup and powder, and her skin looked nearly normal, if still a little yellow and orange in patches.

"There's only so much that makeup can do," Chloe told me quietly, "and I've done it."

"You're a genius," I told her.

She gave an exhausted wave and staggered outside.

The bridesmaids gathered around Brenda and very carefully slipped her into her dress. There was a lot of body makeup to avoid. A quick decision was made to cover her bare and splotchy shoulders with a gauzy shawl. Brenda's cousin suggested we cut down Brenda's long veil and turn it in the other direction and have it be a short face veil instead, but luckily she was hushed up before Brenda could hear her and wonder why she would need a veil if they were all saying she looked fine. Finally, her ten bridesmaids bundled Brenda, a little scabby, streaky, and shaky, but pretty well convinced she was a beautiful bride, off to be married.

If the groom had any second thoughts, he certainly didn't show it. After the ceremony, the guests gathered to congratulate Brenda and tell her how lovely she looked. Sarah and I took careful pictures. When we finished the bridal portraits, Sarah took me aside.

"About your 'no retouching' rule," said Sarah.

"You're thinking this may be a good time to make an exception?"

"Exactly."

"Funny, I was thinking the same thing."

All the way through the reception, as far as the bridesmaids were concerned, Brenda could do no wrong. When she showed a thirty-five-minute slide show of pictures dating back to when she and the groom were in diapers, they sat in the front row and cooed appreciatively at every photo, long after even Brenda's father had grown bored and gone outside to smoke a cigar. And later, when the DJ announced the bouquet toss, in perhaps the greatest show of loyalty of the evening, the only two unmarried women in the room, both of them bridesmaids and well into their thirties, did their best to look thrilled when they joined the six-year-old flower girl in the middle of the empty dance floor and tried to catch the bouquet.

"You know," said Sarah as we headed home late that evening, "those crazy bridesmaids really stepped up when Brenda needed them. I was pretty surprised after the hard time they gave her."

"They were great." I thought about it a bit. "Seems like maybe they figured out the whole dress thing just wasn't so important after all."

Sarah was quiet for a few minutes. Then she laughed. "They sure did look awful, though. That pregnant one was a disaster, and the big one with the curly armpits—that was bad. But no one could have looked good in a dress like that."

"Would you have worn that dress?" I asked her.

"Are you nuts? Not in a million years."

"Not even if it was my wedding?"

"Honey," said Sarah, as she settled in for her usual after-wedding nap, "there's a lot I'd do for you. And if you ever rip off half the skin on your face and turn yourself into a human banana, I'll be right there for you. But don't ever, ever ask me to wear anything that ugly, or you will definitely find yourself with one less ace assistant and drop-dead-fabulous friend."

16

Whipped Cream and a Cherry

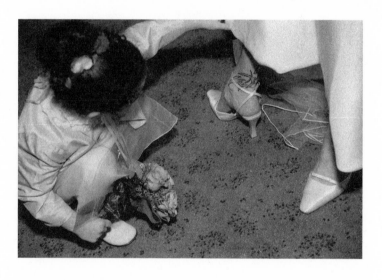

*S*ometimes, when I start telling stories, I think it must seem as though every wedding I photograph features either a crazy person or a disaster. In fact, many of them do. But not all. There are lots of weddings that run smoothly, with beautifully behaved guests, thoughtful clients, and a sense of joyful celebration throughout. I enjoy these hugely, but I'd be lying if I didn't admit that in the long run the crazy stuff is the most interesting. I like crazy, and I like neurotic people. I may now live on the West Coast, but I spent my formative years in New York City—a place where no one is scared of sarcasm and neurosis comes with the territory. Most of my close friends are wonderfully mixed up and confused about life in general and see this as the human condition. Being somewhat crazy, they would say, is a natural response to living in a maddening world. Depression alternating with periods of manic happiness is a perfectly logical reaction to lives that are horribly sad at times and wonderful at others. My friends love to wallow in the downs and celebrate the ups of their lives. They would rather feel than medicate. They think that a little coffee, and even the occasional cigarette, might not be the worst thing in the world. They go for long periods of time without exercise. Like me, they think that crazy is fine. It's normal that worries us. Maybe that's why the world of weddings is a perfectly comfortable place for me to spend a good deal of my time.

Crazy is OK. Even tasteless can have its moments. But vulgar is no fun at all. That word comes to me from my mother. A refugee from Poland during the Second World War, she was raised for most of her life in England. There she absorbed much of the British abhorrence for what she referred to as washing your dirty linen in public. Far from being prudish, she just liked good manners and an absence of bad behavior. When we moved to America, our family learned to live by the far more confessional style of this country, though my mother still maintained a rather British sense of disdain for anything that could be termed vulgar. Crude could be forgiven. The occasional slip of the tongue into bad language was entirely understandable. Sex was open for general discussion. In fact, it was the subject of many mealtime debates in our house, on those evenings when we weren't arguing politics or religion. But there was a line you did not cross. That was vulgarity. I'll give you an example.

The ritual of the garter is an outdated and somewhat crude event. It never seems all that amusing to me to photograph the groom with his head up under the bride's dress as he tries to pull off her garter with his teeth. In the many photographs I have taken of this singularly odd event, the bride almost always has the same look in her eye. She may be laughing, but nine times out of ten you can plainly see she knows that this was a big mistake and that she, an educated, talented, successful woman, has voluntarily placed herself in a ridiculous position. This is sloppy and makes the players look collectively foolish, but it's good-humored and not really vulgar.

On the other hand, there were Kelly and Travis. They were, without doubt, unforgivably, irredeemably vulgar. I was hired by Kelly over the telephone. She and I did not meet until the day of her wedding. It was obvious almost immediately that we were not a good fit. Everyone in the bride's dressing room was getting drunk. They were not having a glass of celebratory champagne, or even a little something to steady the nerves. This was the determined kind of drinking that had a purpose and lacked all joy. The bridesmaids were cracking off-color jokes about what the bride and groom would do later that night. The mother of the bride was sitting in the corner, chain-smoking and ignoring everyone. Outside, it was raining steadily. Above the arch where the happy couple would stand to take their vows, a stream of water spattered down from a gutter. The wedding was taking place at a restaurant, with the ceremony itself in an outside courtyard and the reception and dinner in a tented area. The florist was hysterical. Tired from a wedding the night before, she had parked her van outside the restaurant in time to take a quick nap. Unfortunately, her alarm had not gone off. She didn't wake up until half an hour before the ceremony, when one of the groomsmen started pounding on the window. She was now dashing madly about trying to pin on boutonnieres, put table arrangements in place, and find the bridal bouquet, which had gone missing. The staff of the restaurant looked damp and gloomy, they were busy wiping the soaking-wet chairs and trying to find enough umbrellas to keep the guests dry during the ceremony. The groom was nowhere to be seen. On every table there was a small heart-shaped tin of mints with MINT TO BE TOGETHER printed on the lid in pink.

Eventually a crowd of guests assembled, and the groom and his best man appeared at last. Their eyes were slightly out of focus and a little too bright. The groom was a good-looking man but entirely eclipsed by the best man, who looked both astonishingly handsome and unpleasant. The ceremony began. The bride emerged, a froth of beading, bright white satin, and fire-engine-red lips. Her gown had a huge skirt and a minimal top. The groom slurred his vows. The ceremony was over in a matter of seven damp minutes, and everyone ducked quickly under the white vinyl tent to start drinking in earnest.

I tried to put together some groups for the family photographs that the bride had requested. Not for long. No one was really interested, and I finally gave up. When everyone sat down to dinner, there were toasts. Well, just one. The best man stood up and made a strangely suggestive speech, emphasizing the fact that he personally knew how lucky the groom was. No one seemed to realize how odd this sounded. In fact, no one seemed to be listening. Except the bride. She looked pleased.

During dinner, the groom and best man vanished. The bride chatted with her girlfriends and pretended not to notice. Her anger became increasingly obvious. When the DJ approached her for the fourth time to ask if she would like to have him play the first dance, I thought she might hit him. I took him aside and suggested he stop asking. The first dance never happened. When the groom finally returned, he and the bride fought loudly. The groom was so high that he didn't care; the bride, too angry. The guests ate their dinner and drank. I seemed to be the only one at the wedding who was feeling at all uncomfortable. Of course, that may have been because I was the only one who was sober.

After dinner came the high point. The bride was led out to a chair placed in the middle of the dance floor. Someone produced a large plastic cup, the kind they give you with those humongous sodas at the movies. In the bottom of the cup they put a cherry. The cup was filled with whipped cream from a can and placed between the bride's thighs. Then, one by one, all interested male guests were invited to get on their knees and see if they could "get the bride's cherry." Keeping their hands behind their back and using only their tongue, they each gave it a try. Everyone had a great time. The bride hiked up her dress to hold the cup in her crotch. She loudly encouraged the men to "go deeper." From a visual perspective, this was a gold mine. There were faces smeared with cream. The bride had thrown her head back and was laughing. The men jostled and pushed to be next in line. It looked like the best man would win, but the groom eventually shoved him aside, crushed the cup, and got his prize. The bride vanished into her dressing room to clean up. The groom and best man went with her.

Forty-five minutes later, it was long past time for me to leave, but the door to the dressing room was still shut. I needed to get my coat. When family members pounded on the locked door there was no reply. No one knew what to do, but no one seemed worried. Guests just went up to the door and yelled good-bye through the keyhole. Another fifteen minutes of guests shouting at the door, and it finally opened. The two men were sprawled in chairs looking disheveled and pleased with themselves. Kelly, her mascara smeared and her eyes glassy, was trying to rearrange her dress and clean up the mess her makeup had become. She asked for a cigarette.

I left, quietly. I just wanted to go home, wash my face, and curl up on the couch. I wanted to tell my husband all the reasons that sometimes my work makes me unutterably sad. I maintained my tradition of bringing my daughter one of the wedding favors, and the next morning I gave her a little tin of mints that said MINT TO BE TOGETHER. I tried, as I always do, to think of a funny story to tell her about the wedding. But nothing came to mind.

17

Speed Bumps

When I'm working, there are lots of things that get in my way. Mostly these are human things. All too often, a bride and groom decide that just one type of documentation isn't enough. They need video as well. There I am, moving in quietly to try to capture the first moment of genuine tenderness I've seen between a couple all evening, when two things happen at once: The bride and groom are suddenly bathed in a blinding light, and a huge black microphone is dangling in the top left corner of my shot. The couple freeze like terrified deer in the headlights of an oncoming truck. It's the video guys, and they're being helpful. "Hey, Claire, thought we'd help you out and light things up a bit. Let us know if we get in your way." Of course, they *are* in my way. Everywhere I turn, there they are. Straight down the aisle, up on the altar, circling the groom and his mother on the dance floor like stalkers. Later tonight one of them will probably catch the bouquet when the bride tosses it and then ask me if I got the shot.

There are some good video people out there. They are low-key and creative, don't wear a cheap tux, and are fun to have a glass of wine with at the end of the evening. But they cost a lot. So, though I recommend them and try to explain to my clients the reason it's worth paying more money, I usually end up fighting for floor space with a team from Mega-Video. The Mega-Video guys can make me nuts, but I do have a soft spot for the brains behind the operation. His name is Jeremy Thompson. I should probably explain here that I was born in London. As a result of moving to three different countries before I was ten, I've retained quite a strong accent of some kind. Most people place it as British. Jeremy, after our first phone conversation, had decided I was French. Who knows why he settled on that particular nationality, but for a while it made for some great e-mail.

It all started when my wedding bookings were getting steadily busier. I had interesting and financially stable clients, and many of them were asking me for recommendations for other vendors. The photographer is a great person to ask for a video recommendation. You are far less likely to wind up in the middle of a turf war at your wedding if your photographer and videographer get along. We know who does good work and who won't stick a microphone in people's faces and ask them to say a few cute words about the bride and groom. Photographers can usually tell you which video company is unlikely to send you a video of your wedding set to the tune of "Memories."

In San Francisco, there are lots of people shooting wedding videos, but there is only one Jeremy Thompson. Jeremy's company is huge. Tentacles of the Thompson wedding video empire creep across the state and way outside of it, too. The man is a master of marketing. I happen to know, from chatting with a few of his employees, that Jeremy keeps a computer database with personal details on everyone he deals with. Pet's name, husband's birthday, car make and year, favorite food. I know that if I'm talking on the telephone to Jeremy and he's liberally peppering the conversation with charming personal references, it's because he's looking at a page on his computer screen and doing a quick review of my personal data. I admire the guy. It takes real chutzpah to be that smarmy. There are cracks in the almost flawless methodology of the Jeremy machine, though, and I happen to be one of them. I thought something was a bit odd when, after we first spoke by phone, I had an e-mail from him that started with a jaunty "Bonjour!" He was writing to say merci for a referral and to tell me that he was "beaucoup" excited about the fact that one of his people would have the "tres grand" pleasure of working with me. He did just about everything but wish me Happy Bastille Day. I was confused. Was he French? Was I?

The e-mails continued. The day before any of my weddings that his people would be videotaping, I would get another one. "Bonjour, Claire! We are super beaucoup excited about seeing you tomorrow!" Any referral would bring a charming e-mail saying merci and thanking my charmante self for being so, well . . . charmante, mostly. I started referring clients to his company just because I wanted to see what kind of a message would come next. I blew it, though. I was working a wedding with a young husband-and-wife team that he had sent out to cover the event. I finally couldn't resist asking them what was up with the French love notes I kept getting.

"Aren't you French?" They looked astonished.

"Er, no."

"You're in the database as French. He told us to say something nice about France to you. Are you sure you're not French? Because Jeremy's sure you are."

"Believe me, I'm sure." I thought about this for a moment. I hated the idea of no more international love notes from Jeremy. Then it came to me.

"Could you let Jeremy know I'm not French? But you might want to tell him what I am."

"Sure, yeah, great. What are you? We'll tell him for sure. He really likes to know that stuff."

"Well, actually I'm Polish."

"Wow, really, you're Polish? Man, I don't know if Jeremy speaks any Polish."

It's true, I am Polish. I even have a decent command of the language. It's a difficult one to learn, so I'm not all that surprised that these days I just get polite e-mails from Jeremy's assistant.

*P*hotographing a wedding with a videographer, though it may sometimes be annoying, can also be great if the people involved are talented and thoughtful, and have a sense of humor. I've had some wonderful times working weddings with videographers, and some good laughs, too. It's the extra photographers that I have trouble ever seeing the funny side of. They're the roadblocks that make me really nuts.

Why spend a considerable amount of money to hire a professional photographer you have just jumped through all sorts of hoops to find, interview, and pay for, just to let a crowd of amateurs ruin two-thirds of the pictures?

I don't mean your Uncle Harry. He's not the problem. I don't really mind hearing about how he's a charter member of his local photography club, reads new equipment manuals for fun, and knows more about all sorts of specialty gadgets than I do. I'll even be impressed that the corner coffee shop hosted a solo show of his photographs of spring flowers and that he won a blue ribbon for photography at the state fair. He's not a wedding photographer, though. Or a professional. And he is not being paid to document your wedding. What he is, is in my way. So he needs to be dealt with, but nicely.

Over the years, I have learned to manage Uncle Harry. At any wedding there is always one serious amateur photography buff who views the occasion as an opportunity to really show off his moves. I'm fine with that. I want them to have a good time. Within limits. What I like to do is get them off in a corner for a chat early on. We have a friendly talk about the pros and cons of our various pieces of equipment. Since theirs invariably has more bells and whistles than mine, but I have the advantage of using impressively simple equipment—as in "Boy, you must be really good if you can work with just that"—we both end up feeling fine about ourselves. Then I bring up the ways that they can help me by "staying the hell out of my way," as Sarah likes to say, or, by "working collaboratively with me," which is a more diplomatic way of putting it. That way, I won't mess up his shots and he won't mess up mine. And the bride and groom won't regret inviting him to the wedding. It all works out fine, and Harry turns out to be no problem at all.

The real problem is all the other help I get. With the advent of digital photography, and most especially the dreaded camera in every cell phone, the situation has gotten so out of hand that I find myself having to fight and shove my way through a crowd of cell-phone-waving bodies just to get one clear shot of the bride and groom exchanging their vows. It's a jungle out there.

Technologically, I'm rarely on the cutting edge of things. I don't like gadgets, and my computer and I often disagree about how to do something. The computer wins because I have a temper and end up throwing things. Sometimes I cry, which is embarrassing but true. And then I ask my husband to fix it for me, which is even more embarrassing. I was the last person I know to get a cell phone, and I don't suppose I'll ever start text messaging. But the thing that most people seem to find strangest these days is the fact that I don't want to go digital. I love film. As helpful friends tell me, film sends my costs sky high and comes in little separate rolls of thirty-six frames that you actually have to put in and take out of the camera, for God's sake! Later you have to scan the negatives if you want to alter them in Photoshop and so on. I've heard it all. I'm a dinosaur. Soon no one will hire me. I'm missing the wave, the curve, the moment. I'm doomed. I'm fine with that. I use film for precisely the reasons that others see as shortcomings when compared to digital photography.

I like blur and surprises. And anticipation. It's more fun not knowing exactly what I've captured till later. People praise the sharpness of their digital cameras, but I don't see any reason that things need to be so sharp all the time. To me, the sharpness looks less like a memory. After the age of forty nothing is exactly crystal clear anyway, and lots of things look more interesting with a few fuzzy edges. Having limits on the amount of film I can afford to shoot seems like a good thing, too. Limits inspire creativity. They give you something to push up against and force you to consider the choices you're making. I don't want to correct imperfections in Photoshop. I like crooked teeth and big noses, a veil blowing across a bride's face, eyes squinting up because someone is laughing really hard. The flaws are the good stuff. I think mascara is supposed to run when you cry. Your nose is supposed to get red, too. For goodness sake, what is the point of smoothing life out? I'm happiest wandering around with my manual camera, which feels solid and reliable. I don't want my camera to think for me or make my decisions. What if it's smarter than I am and makes better decisions? I'd rather not know. I smile politely when someone at a wedding asks me when I'm going to upgrade to digital. It's taken me years to downgrade to this point. Why spoil it?

I recently read a comment by an author who was frustrated that a photographer she was watching at a wedding was taking time to put a new roll of film in his camera. Film? Obviously this was a photographer after my own heart who was actually going to the trouble and expense of using film so as to give his clients what he believed was the best result possible. The author sneered at this professional for using film and went on to say that everyone, including blind grandmothers, now shoots digital. How true. But it's safe to assume that most couples would not hire a blind grand-mother to shoot their wedding, no matter how quick she is with a digital camera. Or, if they did, they might not be too happy with the result.

But she had a point. Everyone is taking digital pictures at weddings these days. The church ceremonies are the worst. Often the on-site church coordinator sends me a multipage document to sign weeks before the wedding. I have to prom-ise to dress appropriately, stand where I am told to stand, use no flash, stay out of the aisle, and behave properly. At one San Francisco church, I am simply told that I am permitted to take one picture and one picture only from where they say and when they say I can. So there I will be on the wedding day, not dressed in a bikini or anything else inappropriate, sitting quietly in the back row, my cameras on the pew next to me, as 250 cell-phone-toting and tiny-digital-point-and-shoot-carrying guests find their seats. Within minutes they are in the aisle photographing the bride as she enters. Never mind that to get a glimpse of his intended the groom would need to climb up on the cross.

As the ceremony progresses, guests scramble up on the altar and practically shove the bridesmaids aside to get a good angle. I glance over at the church coordinator. She's watching me like a hawk. I motion hopefully toward all the flashes going off like fireworks and pick up one of my cam-eras as though to suggest I might get just a shot or two of my own given the situation, but she shakes her finger at me. No dice. I must obey the rules. So I sit there, like some highly paid guest at the wedding. Then the bride and groom kiss, the ceremony is officially over, and I am out in the aisle to get a shot as they come back down. Happy, both laughing, they look great. I'm just starting to shoot when a spiderweb of arms crisscrosses my viewfinder. I can't see the couple at all anymore. Every single guest with a cell phone has one arm out in the aisle to get a shot of the bride and groom as they go by.

I'm getting desperate. As the bride and groom go past I turn to follow them and perhaps at least get one nice shot as they walk out through the open church doors. Suddenly I am shoved hard from behind, and a frantic guest pushes past me with his phone at arm's length in front of him.

"'Scuze me, coming through," he mutters. "Look out, I'm filming here."

It seems that you can take movies with those little phones now, too. Who knew? Everyone but me, I guess.

As I see it, if you really want the pictures of your wedding to be the best they possibly can be, skip the videographer, tell Uncle Harry to just enjoy the day and leave his "work" at home, and ask your guests to let the photographer do her job. In other words, clear the road.

18

I Do

$\mathcal{W}$e were sitting out on the deck one day, watching the turkey vultures dry their wings. They do this by sitting in a row on a fence and spreading their wings out wide to catch the sun. Their black silhouettes looked terrifying the first time I saw them. Something out of a Hitchcock film. No, nothing so classy, more like a cheap horror movie. The first sign of the coming of Satan, that sort of thing. It was only a matter of time till the plague of locusts descended and the devil spawn arrived.

Luckily, the landlord was at home, and he explained what I was looking at before my paranoia spiraled totally out of control. The world would survive another day. The landlord was pretty helpful in other ways, too. He was the one who came out with a hose and sprayed the wild turkeys off the roof of our house the day I was afraid to come out while they were all sitting up there waiting to ambush me. It might seem odd that I was afraid of a bunch of turkeys, but these were wild turkeys, and believe me, you would have been, too. They once attacked the headlights of our pickup truck as we tried to drive down our steep dirt driveway. When my husband got out of the car to shoo them away, they rushed him. Terrified, he dashed back to the car, threw himself inside, and slammed the door on what looked like a dozen rabid turkeys determined to finish us off. After that I felt vindicated. I'd taken some ribbing about the turkeys-on-the-roof incident.

But now we were somewhat acclimated. The vultures drying their wings were just part of the scenery, spotting the occasional rattlesnake when we were hiking was still scary, but not cause to run for home, Stalker Dog was down in the yard peacefully sleeping her old age away in the sun, and we were talking marriage.

"So, think we should get married?"

"I don't know. Do you?"

"I do. Do you want to?"

"I do."

"I do, too."

"We should, then."

"Definitely."

"We could have a baby."

"I'd like to have your baby."

"You would?"

"Absolutely."

"Let's get married, then."

"It'll be great."

No declarations. Not really even a very big deal. It was just the logical next step in what had started on that airplane. Except something didn't feel right.

A few days after our talk on the deck, we were driving along in the truck, Stalker Dog lying between us with her head in my sort-of-fiancé's lap. We were headed out to the beach to make Stalker take a walk. We always told her it was going to be fun, and she always slumped around protesting she'd rather stay exactly where she was, lying half asleep in the sun. We'd drag her off to the beach, she'd limp around for a while complaining that she had sand in her paws and the water was too cold, and we'd eventually call it a day and take her home to sleep again. Stalker was an East Coast dog and far too old to learn to romp on California beaches. But here we were, winding our way along Highway 1 and trying one more time to convince her that the beach would be fun.

"So are we doing this marriage thing or not?" I suddenly asked. It sounded a little angry. Where did that come from? John looked surprised.

"I thought so, yes. Don't you want to?"

"Well, you don't seem to really care about it." What? Who was saying this stuff? It got worse. "You didn't even bother to propose." It was quiet in the car for a moment.

"You want a proposal?"

"Yes, I want a proposal. I want you to surprise me and ask me to marry you like you aren't really sure I'll say yes. You also need to tell me why you want me to marry you."

"But you already said yes. I mean, we agreed."

Agreed? I didn't want to agree. I wanted to be asked. Properly.

"It's not supposed to be an agreement like deciding what to have for dinner! It's supposed to be, I don't know, bigger than that. Or something." I had no idea what I meant, and the fact that I didn't even know why I cared about this made me even angrier.

"Forget it. If you don't want to propose, you don't have to." I slumped in the corner.

John looked over at me. He scratched Stalker behind the ears. Then he smiled. "Don't worry," he said.

And then I didn't.

Two days later, he proposed. Properly. We sat on some rocks by the ocean, and he told me exactly why he wanted to marry me and waited to see if I would say yes. I said yes. He gave me a lovely silver bracelet, and we went out to dinner and drank champagne. I was engaged. I couldn't tell you why I needed that proposal, but I did. Though it seemed almost a foregone conclusion that he and I would spend the rest of our lives together, I still wanted the moment to be marked in some way. Whatever this was going to be, we would not slip into it casually. We'd be wide-awake. We would pay attention.

*N*ow we had a wedding to plan, and neither of us had any idea what to do about it. We'd only recently moved across the country, so all our family and friends were back on the other coast, and my almost husband had already been through a huge, very conventional, and very elaborate wedding once. A wedding where he had been told early in the process to sit back, keep quiet, and "let the women do the planning." He didn't want a repeat of that, and I didn't know what I wanted. So we called my brother and told him our news. He did exactly what a very good and extremely kind older brother who knows his sister very well and is happy to see her making a really good decision for a change should do. He said to leave it to him.

While I was careening around from one uncertain method of survival to another, my brother had followed a more linear course. Though by nature more of a dreamer than a businessman, he was determined not to live with the financial insecurity that we had all suffered from as children. He first obtained a philosophy degree and then became a lawyer. Along the way he married a lovely Southern woman, and they now had three children, a busy, happy life, and a huge old Victorian house in upstate New York from which my brother commuted every day to his law firm in Manhattan. They had money, time, and generosity of spirit. And they were throwing us a wedding.

We couldn't have wished for a better solution. We would arrive at our own wedding almost as guests ourselves. We didn't care about what sort of flowers there would be, if we'd have round tables or square, or what flavor cake we should have. What mattered to us both was to not think about those things at all. All I wanted was to invite the sixty or so people we cared most about and have my brother and my sister hold my hands and walk me down to wherever my guy was standing. Oh, and I needed a dress. That turned out to be easy.

Since John's taste in clothes was sometimes rather better than mine, we ignored the taboo that says the groom should not see the bride's dress and went together to a shop downtown where things were just too expensive enough to make it feel like something special was going on. I tried on the first dress we both liked. It fit, and we were done. We bought our plane tickets, sent out invitations, and—apart from a brief flurry when we had to find someone who would be willing to put up with Stalker Dog's eccentricities while we were away—we were worry-free. Even that turned out to be all right because we met Susan, who took one look at Stalkey and read her like a book.

"I see the food's the fun?" she said, a less than polite reference to our dog's expanding waistline. Then she said, "Nothing wrong with that at her age," and fed her a biscuit. Stalker gave an appreciative wag, and we were good to go. We arrived at our wedding prepared to love everything, and we did.

19

Can You Be Rich and Funny?

$\mathcal{E}$very morning I go for a walk. Fueled by caffeine, I climb up and down the hills of my San Francisco neighborhood. When I finally reach the top of the highest hill, I stop, panting, and take a look at the swathe of city spread out at my feet. For a few minutes I feel like I'm seventeen again and can leap tall buildings in a single bound. I need that feeling more and more lately because I've been noticing something odd. Certain people in my life who are supposed to be older, and therefore wiser, than I am are now younger. My doctor looks like a kid, and my lawyer definitely doesn't seem old enough to be giving me advice about anything. Then there's the money. How do my clients get so much money at such an early age? How do they get so much money at all? These days one shiny Lexus SUV or Range Rover after another is pulling up in my driveway. Out hop a couple of well-dressed twenty-six or -seven-year-olds coming to discuss the sixty-, eighty-, or hundred-thousand-dollar wedding that they are paying for by themselves. I've tried to figure it out, but when I ask them what sort of work they do, they just look up from their handheld wireless devices and mutter, "Finance," as though that explains everything. Perhaps it does.

I have found that there is an equation relating to twenty-somethings with lots of money that almost never fails to be true. Obviously, it's totally unfair to make generalizations—but so what? It goes like this: More money equals less humor. Take Spencer and Diane. Actually, you have to take Spencer, Diane, and Pat, the wedding planner, since they were never without her. My first impression of Pat was that she should be teaching an obedience class to dogs, or perhaps coaching a football team somewhere. There was a lot of her, and all of her looked stern and solid. Cheeky corgi or disgruntled linebacker, Pat would be able to handle it. She was dressed in no-nonsense navy blue jacket, beige pants, sensible shoes, and just the right amount of chunky gold jewelry. Sitting down on the least comfortable chair in my living room, she took a notebook out of her briefcase, opened it, and looked up expectantly.

Spencer and Diane were so poised that it made me feel I should sit up straighter, or maybe beg them both to slump a little. Both were in perfect shape, happily aware of their own glowing good health, sensible dietary habits, and impressive workout schedule. They had matching North Face jackets and tans. Settling themselves onto the couch, they adjusted their hair and smiles and tried for a little small talk.

"We left Waldo outside," said Diane. "You can see him if you look out the window."

I had a look. The golden retriever sitting in the backseat

of the shiny red BMW convertible parked in my driveway looked like he had been ordered from the Ralph Lauren catalog.

"Nice dog," I said, because he was.

Pat cleared her throat and called the meeting to order.

"We need to talk about the romantics," she said and looked at Spencer.

"Right, Pat, thank you." Spencer nodded, obviously happy that the small talk was over. Enough about the incidentals; time to get down to the business of Spencer and Diane. "What are your specific thoughts on the romantics, Claire?" he asked. He and Diane looked at me, waiting for an answer. So did Pat, eyebrows raised. I felt like a kid who'd forgotten to do her homework.

"Romantics? I think we should definitely do some." Not exactly an impressive answer, but it had the virtue of sounding like I knew what the hell they were talking about.

"Yes, obviously," Spencer said impatiently. "We're trying to be a little more specific here, Claire. We've set aside two hours to do our romantics. Will that be enough?"

"Well, my husband and I can do ours in considerably less time than that," I told him, "but it's always nice to have extra time to improvise, right?" OK, so it was a pretty dumb joke.

Spencer and Diane stared at me blankly. Pat stopped writing and looked up.

"Romantic pictures, Claire," she explained dryly and scribbled something in her notebook.

I could just imagine it. *Photographer makes stupid joke. Do not recommend to clients in future.*

"Oh, right. I actually knew that." I was feeling a bit testy. I decided to ask a few questions of my own. "What location were you thinking of, Diane? For the romantics, I mean."

Spencer answered. Apparently Diane preferred to let him do the talking. She helped by nodding a lot.

"We toured the Sonoma town square with Pat and identified the best locations," said Spencer. "Of course, we'd defer to your judgment on that, Claire." Pat looked up from her notepad and cleared her throat.

Right. In my dreams.

"We'd like to have some spontaneous pictures taken of me feeding Diane an ice-cream cone in a lighthearted way," continued Spencer.

Pat spoke without looking up from her notepad. "Vanilla, Spencer."

Diane nodded vigorously. The dress! Stains!

"Vanilla. Good thinking, Pat. Make a note of that," said Spencer. Pat made a note.

"We'd also like shots of the two of us seated in a crowded café with all the other customers looking at us. We'd be looking at each other, of course. Also, shots crossing a busy street with someone stopping the traffic. Pat, set that up, please." Pat made a note. Probably something along the lines of *SWAT team needed at plaza. 2:00 P.M.*

Spencer was still talking. "After that we'd leave it up to you, Claire. Well, except for the list of park shots, the playful stuff at the old movie theater marquee, and the specific vineyard shots at the reception site. How does that sound?"

"Lovely," I said. "Just out of curiosity, what are your

guests doing during the two hours we're shooting the spontaneous romantics?"

"Great question, Claire," said Spencer.

Next he'd be patting me on the head and saying, "Atta girl." Good thing Sarah wasn't here. She'd need to be restrained. Even I was beginning to lose it a little.

"Glad you liked it, Spence." I said. Pat looked up from her notepad. Surprisingly, I caught a glimpse of humor in the look she gave me. Perhaps I hadn't read Pat quite right.

Spencer was oblivious. It was his world, and he was busy organizing it.

"We have that covered, Claire," he said. "They will be having dancing lessons. We don't want anyone to be embarrassed, and it's important for the pictures that our guests look good dancing."

"You're worried about how your friends will look when they're dancing?" This was a new one.

"Not worried." Spencer looked pained. "Concerned. We want them to feel confident and to be able to fully enjoy the experience we're providing for them. We've hired a very expensive salsa band."

"Very expensive," echoed Pat.

Diane nodded.

Spencer excused himself to go have a private moment with his BlackBerry. The room seemed quiet without him. Suddenly Diane spoke up.

"The romantics are very, very important to us, Claire. Also, during the wedding we really want you to concentrate on Spencer and me and not get distracted by the guests. If you stay close and take pictures of us, then you can be sure you won't miss anything important. That would be best. I mean, we do care about our friends and our families, but it's really our day. I'm sure that the pictures of us will be the ones we'll care about most in the future. Probably that's what all your couples say, right?"

I suspected I was not going to be able to fully enjoy the experience that Spencer and Diane were going to provide for me. I let Pat answer.

"You're completely right, Diane," she said. "No one wants pictures of their family or their guests."

Diane nodded.

Then Pat looked at me and winked.

20

Human Error, or When Bad Things Happen to Good Photographers

It's what I call the once-in-a-lifetime problem. As brides have variously put it to me: "Don't forget, it's our once-in-a-lifetime day." "The pictures are the most important part for us because when it's all over that's all we'll have to remind us of our once-in-a-lifetime event." I have nightmares about this. No film, forgot the camera, can't find batteries in my bag—that sort of nightmare. Compared to this, the angry-bulldog ring bearer or the wedding planner turned crazed dictator is nothing. The thing is, I can't control the weather on your wedding day, so you can't blame me if it rains. I'm not responsible for the cake that melts, the dress that fits horribly, or the groom who behaves badly. I can, and do, keep my cameras in perfect shape, bring extras of everything, and triple-check my bag before I go out to work. But it's a part of natural law that things will go wrong sometimes. It may not be my fault, but I'll definitely get blamed. And then there's nothing to shelter me from the wrath of the client except a huge apology, a refund—and running for cover.

*V*ery soon after our cross-country move, I realized my photography career had taken a nosedive. I'd left a good client base and lots of steady work back east, and it was going to take me a while to get new clients in California. I decided to set up several days of portrait sittings at a friend's studio in New Jersey. A few phone calls, a mailing, and it was all arranged. I'd get a cheap plane ticket, shoot fifteen portrait sittings in four days, see some friends, and head home again. A work marathon. I was looking forward to it. And that's exactly how it went. It was a huge success. I came home, tired but very happy, with seventy-five rolls of shot film in my bag. I took them straight to my lab to have them developed.

The next day the phone rang. It was the lab. The film was blank. All of it. Not a single picture anywhere. I sat on the floor and sobbed. Fifteen portrait sittings. All those people who had trusted me to catch their baby's first tooth, kid's new haircut, grandmother at ninety-four—and there was nothing. They had come with their children dressed up in new outfits, arranged to miss work or school, changed naptimes and family plans to accommodate me. And with each of those families I had spent time, energy, and imagination. We had run around pulling funny faces to make some babies laugh or sat waiting while others napped or nursed. We had coaxed the family dog to smile and cheered when everyone looked at the camera at exactly the same moment for that one perfect shot. And the film was all blank. And they had given me checks. Fifteen of them.

I eventually learned that my beloved old medium-format camera had suffered from heatstroke. In the intense temperatures of the New Jersey summer, something had gone gooey and the lens had become stuck in the open position. Because in a twin-lens camera you are not looking directly through the lens, I had no way of knowing that every time I pressed the shutter release, nothing was happening. I heard the satisfying click of the button and assumed all was well.

Now I had fifteen phone calls to make and an awful lot of apologizing to do. I ended up flying back again and re-shooting almost all of the portraits. Everyone was kind, and I considered myself lucky. One thing about portrait sittings, you can almost always go and have another try. And therein lies the Big Event problem. The terror of the once-in-a-lifetime screwup. If something goes wrong, it has gone wrong for good.

In the town back east where I first shot weddings, there is a famous university, and affiliated with that university is an equally famous institute—we'll just call it the Institute for Exceptionally Brilliant People—and it is, as you can imagine, populated by clever people, some of whom are quite famous. One of these exceptional people asked me if I would photograph a very special once-in-a-lifetime event. It was a family reunion. The party would be held at the institute, and the many generations of this distinguished family would be flying in from all over the world for the celebration. Some of them would be meeting for the first and only time in their lives. Many were extremely old, and to make the long trip from their various native countries would be a huge effort for them. Not surprisingly, the photographs of this gathering would be enormously important as a histori-cal record for the family. I happily accepted the job. The event was lovely. There were speeches, toasts, beautiful mo-ments of reunion and tears. I took many, many photographs, conscious of the fact that these would be sent all over the world as a record of this day. Then I went home to process the film.

In those days, I was living in my old converted factory. I'd had a friend frame out and drywall a room in one corner that I set up as a darkroom. It was the perfect live/work space. I had barely any furniture. A huge black table a friend had loaned me could, when I dragged in the old wooden benches from an abandoned picnic table in the backyard, fit fourteen people for impromptu meals. My bed was an ancient thing that had belonged to my sister-in-law's grandmother. It had an ornate metal frame with flaky old cream-colored paint. I did a whole series of portraits in that bed. I told the people they could wear and do whatever they wanted. I had people in pajamas, bikinis, business suits, and no clothes at all. They chose to eat, sleep, and paint pictures. They brought along pets, friends, stuffed animals, a barbe-cue. I have no idea what the point of it was, but we had a great time. Perhaps that was the point. It was a space where I could play and take whatever sorts of pictures I wanted with no one looking over my shoulder. A place I could start to be happy again.

In the factory, my upstairs neighbor and I threw huge parties. The whole space would fill with dancing bodies, and the table would be piled with food and flowers. I read all day if I wanted to, practiced aikido, and spent hours and hours in the darkroom playing music and watching my work take shape in the chemicals. I loved the darkroom. I would go in and print all night and come out bleary-eyed and pleasantly zoned out from the fumes. I'd have my morning coffee on the back steps watching my old dog search for her beloved and often missing tennis ball.

So I was feeling pretty good about heading into the darkroom with the twenty rolls of film I had shot at the reunion. Processing film is nowhere near as much fun as printing, but with the right music, and if you get into the rhythm of the work, there is something very satisfying about standing in the pitch dark and using a can opener to pop open the film canisters. You slide the film out and roll it onto reels, using your sense of touch to make sure the film is circling on smoothly because you know that any kink or twisted place could ruin your pictures. Then you slip the reels into a metal can and put the lid on. The film is safe inside, and you are free to turn on the lights. Next you pour in a series of chemicals through a light-tight opening in the top of the can, and with each new chemical you turn the can upside down and back upright again with a smooth roll of your wrist for a certain number of minutes. You have to develop, stop developing, and fix the images before you can safely expose your negatives to the light.

I'd done it hundreds of times. By now I had such a physical memory of the steps that I could chat on the phone, dance around, or let myself get distracted in any number of ways and the film was still neatly wound up on the reels and properly processed. But this time I was trying something new. A photographer friend had loaned me two new developing tanks. I was curious to try them out. They were different from the tanks I was used to and held twice as many reels. Instead of the usual four reels, these tanks each held eight. I was pretty excited about this. It's all very well to say that film developing can have a pleasantly meditative quality, but it can also get boring. I'm not a very patient person, and something that could cut my time in half sounded great. I flicked off the lights and got busy.

The new reels were plastic, rather than metal like the ones I habitually used. It took me a while to get the hang of it, but fairly soon I had eight rolls of film loaded into one tank and eight into the other. Sixteen rolls at once! Practically the whole job would be done in one round of developing. This was great. All I needed to do was put the lids on and start pouring the chemicals. Before I got started I flicked on the lights to make sure everything on those unfamiliar new reels looked OK. It took me just a couple of seconds to realize what I'd done. I spun around, hit the light switch, and stood very still in the dark. It may only have been a few seconds, but I knew it was enough. In spite of the fact that I tried to make a deal with whoever is in charge of these sorts of things by promising to be good forever if only the film could be fine, it was all ruined. I went to see the nice man at the institute. When I told him what had happened, he cried.

I still processed my own film after that. Very slowly, in my old four-reel tanks. It was one of those mistakes you only make once. Human error. It's the hardest thing to explain away, to the client and to yourself—especially when every time you shoot it's a once-in-a-lifetime event.

21

Geek Wedding

*Y*ou just call out the names on the shot list as usual, Sarah, and I'll shoot the family stuff as fast as possible." Sarah and I were at our regular meeting place, the corner table at our favorite café. I moved on quickly. "When we get to the reception—"

Sarah interrupted me. She has an uncanny ability to smell a rat. "Can I see the shot list?"

"I'll show you later. Now, at the reception we'll both—"

"Whoa there, planner." Sarah cut me off. "How about I take a look at that shot list right now?"

Too bad. I handed it over. Sarah sat reading for a few minutes. She looked up from the page and stared at me silently for a moment.

"Is this your idea of a joke?" she finally asked. I had to admit that it was. Sarah started to read from the list. It didn't go well.

"Bi`nh, Ngu, Qua^n, Huye^`n, Ha?i." She thought for a minute. "Vietnamese?"

"Bingo." I was laughing. I'd been hoping to blindside her with this one. A few months back we'd done an Indian wedding, and watching Sarah reduce the guests to hysterical laughter with her mangled reading of the family names had been great. The pictures took forever, but everyone looked really happy in them, and I got a terrific shot of Sarah looking sheepish as the great-grandmother shook her finger at her and told her she was hopeless. I had given her a framed copy. Just a little wedding photographer humor. Big mistake. Now Sarah shot me a disgusted look. My timing was way off. She and I had been going through a bad patch lately. It happens in every relationship.

"You'll be the one reading this, kiddo." She went off to get another cup of coffee without offering to get me one. A bad sign. We'd been working too many weekends in a row, and on top of everything else I'd been foolish enough to snap at Sarah a few times when the stress got out of hand and she didn't happen to be right beside me when I needed her. I always apologized later, but that didn't necessarily set things to rights. We needed some fun. Sarah came back and sat down. It was time to make amends.

"Want to shoot a geek wedding with me?"

"A what?"

"Geek wedding. I'll let you have three guesses what the entertainment will be."

Sarah thought it over. "Robot making? That's all I can come up with."

Good guess. But no.

"Board games," I said. "They're really excited about it."

Sarah started to laugh. "You mean like Monopoly, Scrabble, that sort of board games?"

"You bet. To quote the bride and groom, they are planning to have 'a wide and stimulating variety of challenging board games.' And goody bags."

"Goody bags. Like at a kids' party?"

"Yup. But these goody bags will contain a game of some sort dealing with mathematical probabilities. Or something like that. The guests are supposed to solve it. I didn't quite get how it works."

"That's this weekend?" Sarah looked happier.

"Uh-huh, and it gets better. There's no shot list. There are no family group pictures at all. Best of all, the bride let her mother order a dress for her over the Internet and says she doesn't give a damn what she wears because it's going to be the first time any of her friends have seen her in a dress anyway and just seeing their faces is all she cares about."

Now Sarah looked a lot happier. "My kind of bride," she said. We raised our lattes in a toast to brides who don't give a damn what they look like. We were both looking forward to the weekend for a change.

*A*s you've probably gathered by now, quite a few of my couples can be problematic. It's just the nature of the business. But some I love. Gina and Conrad had been a joy from the start.

"I'm shaped like a pear," said Gina, stating the obvious. "Conrad came with me to watch me try on a bunch of wedding dresses today. It was a total riot. They either slip right down me or won't go down at all. One saleslady said I had no waist whatsoever, and another one looked like she was going to start crying after about the tenth dress. Conrad thought it was hysterical. We just did it for a joke anyway, since my mom will find something for me."

"Plus, they kept bringing out white dresses. Little late for that, right?" Conrad cracked up.

"We're mathematicians," said Gina. "So we're very logical. We know what works. Do I look like a poufy-taffeta-dress girl to you?" She didn't. "We don't really have time for this anyway. We're pretty busy. I'm starting a new job in D.C. right after the wedding, and it's so classified I can't even get them to tell me what I'll be doing. Conrad has invented a computer program that does something medical. Only four people besides Conrad can understand it so far."

"I'm a genius," said Conrad. This time they both cracked up.

"The wedding is going to be totally great," said Conrad. "Super-short ceremony and then tons of board games. And swing dancing. Gina and I met swing dancing. She's incredible. All our friends play board games and go swing dancing, so it'll be perfect. Will you come and take the pictures?"

"Absolutely. I wouldn't miss it. Kind of good about the swing dancing, though. I was a bit worried about the visuals. Not a whole lot of action if everyone is playing board games."

"You don't know our friends," said Conrad.

$\mathscr{B}$oy, was he right. These people were maniacs. As soon as Gina, in a red dress with funky 1920s shoes, and Conrad, in a Hawaiian shirt and board shorts, had said their vows, Conrad shouted, "Let the games begin." The goody-bag game involved theoretical problem solving and predicting mathematical probabilities. It was obvious. At least, that's what a group of guests told me. As far as I could tell, each guest got a brown paper bag with poker chips in it. The winner at the end of the evening would be the one with the most poker chips. The point was to get other people's chips by any means necessary. And they did. They gambled for them, thumb-wrestled for them, and stole them. They threw them in the pool and debated the odds on who would jump in the pool first to get them. They pulled out laptops and calculated the probability of success or failure of the guests who were in the lead. They tossed poker chips in the air and debated exactly which guest had the best chance of catching them based on the height, body weight, and angle of flight of the jumpers. They lied, cheated, and sumo-wrestled for them. It was great. In between tackling each other for poker chips, they played knock-down, drag-out games of Scrabble. They played dominoes to the death. And they danced. Every time someone did a particularly wild dance move or flipped a partner upside down, a shower of poker chips would fall. Then the dance floor would flood with guests looking like five-year-olds rushing an exploding piñata. At the end of the evening they counted up everyone's chips. The winner got—you guessed it—a selection of board games.

In the car on the way home, Sarah fished a few stray poker chips out of her camera bag. "All weddings should be like that," she sighed happily. "By the way, did I mention I've been practicing my Vietnamese? I might have a try at that list after all."

We were back on track.

22

A Baby, and More Panic

$\mathcal{O}$ur wedding was over and our move a thing of the past. Things felt too quiet. Wanting to do my bit to keep life interesting, I got pregnant. I lost my appetite for any food that wasn't white and started to worry. What was I doing here? Wearing overalls. Pregnant, of all things. Why wasn't I traveling somewhere with a backpack, my camera, and no responsibilities? How was I going to travel once the baby was born? Do good mothers take newborns hiking in the Himalayas? Do good mothers leave newborns behind and go hiking in the Himalayas alone? John told me everything would be all right. We'd still be us, but us with a baby. It would be great. I wasn't so sure. I hadn't taken a picture I was proud of in months.

I have photographed many pregnant women. Though I do not subscribe to the romantic notion that the bodies of all pregnant women are beautiful simply because the state of pregnancy is a wondrous thing, I do think that it can be an extraordinary time to be photographed. America gives little leeway to women in the realm of physical beauty. The ideal is constantly held up for comparison, and most of us fall woefully short. Pregnancy is one of the few times when we can relax into being less than perfect. We can enjoy a few lovely and useful bulges. Unless, of course, we check out those pictures of pregnant celebrities who seem to have perfectly formed bodies with a small bowling ball applied to the front. The reality is not considered magazine worthy. Hard work is being done, and you usually look like it.

You'd think, having photographed all those naked tummies filled to bursting, I would have been more than ready to love my own pregnant self, but I was no more prepared than anyone else for the upheaval of pregnancy. I was tired. The smell of the manure in the fields of the surrounding farms made me want to be sick. I got fired from the Thomas Kinkade gallery because the owner said she doubted the sincerity of my appreciation for the work. Hard to believe it took her three months to figure that out. My darkroom from back east was in crates somewhere, and I would have had nowhere to reassemble it anyway, even if all sorts of helpful people hadn't already told me how harmful the chemicals would be to my baby. At the local grocery store, the cashier told me that babies were scarred for life by the usual hospital birthing methods and I had better find a doula and set up my home birthing program. In the town, in the park, I saw women breast-feeding children who looked old enough to be making their own lunches. Many people reminded me of the need to let nothing but cloth diapers touch my baby's skin, and at the pediatrician's office I was given a flyer telling me to attend a class on making my own organic baby foods if I did not want to poison my infant with horrific chemicals. Clearly, I was supposed to do an awful lot of things properly. If I didn't, there would be serious consequences. I panicked some more.

Then none of it mattered at all, because, in a rush bright with lights, pain, and the sounds of an emergency in progress, my daughter arrived. She was very early. I heard a doctor say there was no heartbeat. John's face was white as he bent over my bed while they wheeled me to surgery. Someone gave me a paper to sign. Someone took off my wedding ring. A doctor I had never seen before said that they would do all they could. There was no anesthesiologist, and I would have to have an emergency C-section without being put to sleep. I remember wondering if that was allowed. Wouldn't they need to cut me? Wouldn't that hurt an awful lot? And what on earth was happening to my baby? Someone ran into the room. They would put me to sleep after all. I went out.

I woke in a quiet room. A nurse brought me a tiny ball of blanket and put it in my arms. We had a four-pound six-ounce daughter, and she was fine.

The first year of a new and very tiny baby in your life is like an extended underwater swim. I felt as though I existed on another plane from my fellow mortals. I was constantly tired, distracted, and busy. Often I was excruciatingly bored. At bedtime I didn't know what I had been doing all day, just that I never stopped doing something. In my spare lucid moments I felt as though I would never be able to have a sustained period of clear thought again. Accomplishing—or even imagining—any kind of creative effort was mind-boggling. Though deeply moved by the miracle that was my daughter, and capable of spending long periods of time obsessed with the minutiae of her daily needs, or simply staring at a minuscule toenail or examining a tiny ear, I came to realize that I was obviously not going to be someone who felt satisfied immersing herself solely in the creative act of mothering. Somewhere in a storage space, my darkroom equipment was packed in boxes. My life as a photographer seemed to have been packed and stored away, too. I loved my husband and my baby, and I mourned my work.

So we made a decision to move and save my sanity. Within weeks John had been offered a job with an Internet start-up and we were moving to San Francisco. We were suddenly discussing a brave new world of stock options and initial public offerings. We folded imaginary fortunes up like paper airplanes and sent them flying off into the outer realms of possibility. And we would be in a city again. I would perhaps find kindred spirits among other new mothers there, and the long hours of playground time would be less dull. We'd get a babysitter and try some new restaurants, go dancing, see some opera and check out what was going on in the galleries and museums. My restlessness would be absorbed by the energy of being back in a city. I'd throw out the overalls I had worn when pregnant and continued to wear for too long afterward. Perhaps I'd even start photographing again. So we moved. And, briefly, our plan worked.

23

Wine Country Elvis

I'm not an Elvis fan myself. My idea of wedding entertainment would be the best band I could find. For some people, though, Elvis is king, and finding an Elvis is the key to wedding bliss. If you get married in Vegas, finding your own Elvis is probably pretty easy. I imagine they have their own listing in the yellow pages. In Sonoma County, the pickings are much slimmer. At least, that's the only excuse I can come up with for what happened to Chad and Maureen.

I'd never met either of them. Maureen had e-mailed from New York, where she and Chad were both employed doing something that sounded lucrative. "We help connect idea people with financing people" was how Maureen put it. They were having a small wine country wedding and wanted just a few hours of pictures. I don't usually take on small weddings that require a ninety-minute drive each way, but sometimes it's fun to shoot a short one and I didn't have anything else booked, so I said sure. When the shot list of family pictures arrived in the mail, there was a note from Maureen: *There will be a surprise at 8:00 P.M. Chad doesn't know about it. Make sure you have your camera pointed at him a few minutes before eight. I won't tell you about it because then you can enjoy the surprise, too.*

I immediately thought of Sarah. She loves surprises at weddings because they almost always go wrong. I gave her a call.

"Want to come up to Sonoma next weekend and shoot a three-hour wedding with me?"

"Since when do you need help with a three-hour wedding?"

"I don't, but the bride has a surprise for the groom and won't tell me what it is."

There was a pause.

"Will you buy me dinner?"

I figured it would be worth it just to have her along on this one. "Absolutely."

"OK, I'm in. But it better be a good surprise. If it's just some bozo friend of his popping out of the wedding cake, I won't be happy."

So here we were, one week later, at ten to eight. Chad and Maureen had both turned out to be easygoing people, and so far everything had been straightforward. Since it was almost surprise time, I was keeping Chad in sight while Sarah kept an eye on the door. We figured whatever it was, it was probably coming in that way. Sure enough, the door opened, the lights suddenly dimmed, and a fanfare blasted out over the speakers. There was a sad little puff of blue smoke, and when it cleared, there stood Elvis.

Well, sort of. It must have been Elvis because Chad screamed, "Elvis, my man! I can't believe you got me Elvis," and swept Maureen into a huge hug. Everyone cheered. Sarah looked at me. I could tell she was glad she'd come. There in the doorway stood Chad's Elvis wearing a tight white jumpsuit unzipped to his navel and aviator sunglasses, his lip curled in a sneer. Around his waist was a macramé belt woven with multicolored beads. He was no more than five foot one, with matching mops of black hair on his head and chest. The band struck up "Viva Las Vegas." Elvis started to swivel his hips, and Sarah lost it.

"Oh, no, look at his pants. Look at his pants." Sarah was choking.

"What is that? That's not funny. Seriously, Sarah, what the hell is that?"

"Socks—or baseballs or oranges or balloons." Sarah was hysterical now.

"OK, OK. I get it. Go get a drink of water or something." I actually wasn't in much better shape than Sarah now. Elvis had gone in for a little physical enhancement, and whatever it was down there, it shifted around dangerously while he shook his hips. Sometimes Elvis went one way and his crotch another. The effect was mesmerizing. He started "Love Me Tender," and the bride and groom began their first dance. Elvis joined them in a three-way hug. Chad was in heaven. Then, singing away, Elvis turned his back on the audience and, taking advantage of the fact that the crowd would be watching the couple dance, took some time to adjust his manliness. Probably even he had realized that he'd been a bit too ambitious this time. The song ended, and Elvis began his third and final number, a rockin' version of "Heartbreak Hotel." That's when things got ugly.

"Oh, Elvis baby, kiss me." The cry went out from the table of happily drunk middle-aged aunts. Elvis knew his cue when he heard it. He headed right over.

"Close your mouth, sweetheart," he said to one hefty aunt who appeared ready to devour him whole. She closed her mouth, and Elvis swooped in for a big sloppy kiss. Sarah gagged. After that it was chaos. Everyone wanted a kiss from Elvis, a picture with Elvis, a chance to pat him on the bottom.

"I'd do this for free," said Sarah.

"You are," I reminded her. "How about a little help here? I've got to reload, and the line for getting your picture taken with Elvis is out the door."

"I'm on it. Just promise me I'll get copies of these shots."

So Sarah and I worked it. We got pictures of every aunt in almost every conceivable form of embrace with Elvis. We were right there when Elvis swept the scarf from around his neck and ostentatiously wiped the sweat from his brow. He took the bedraggled piece of damp silk and draped it around the bride's neck. She loved it. They all did. They couldn't get enough of that pint-sized Elvis.

Later in the evening, when Elvis had left the building and toasts were being made, Chad took the microphone and put his arm around Maureen. "See this lady here? This is the love of my life. How can you not love a woman who gets you Elvis for your wedding?" The crowd toasted Maureen.

*T*he guests were busy eating dinner, and Sarah and I were just considering a well-deserved glass of wine, when she nudged me in the ribs.

"Elvis is back."

"Where?"

"Check out the little guy by the door."

It was true. Standing just inside the door, looking both furtive and annoyed, was Elvis. But a changed Elvis. No white suit. No glasses. It was Elvis in khaki pants and an Izod shirt.

"Where's his mojo?" Sarah giggled. "Ate the oranges? Popped the balloons? No, wait, I know, he's wearing three pairs of sweat socks on each foot."

"Give the guy a break. Let's go see what he wants."

We wandered over. Elvis looked unhappy.

"Hey, do you guys know who I get paid by?" he whined. "I mean, no one's paid me yet, and I need to get paid maybe sometime this year!"

"Oh, where is the Elvis of yesteryear, or at least his pants?" said Sarah in my ear.

"I think you should probably ask the bride since she's the one who hired you, um, Elvis," I said.

"Please! It's Larry. I don't like being called Elvis when I'm out of character. Obviously. This is so tacky. I shouldn't have to ask like this. Oh, sure, they all love you till it's time to pay."

Elvis was starting to bug me. He was spoiling the magic. Sarah and I headed to the bar. Elvis could sort out his own payroll problems.

"Tough life, show business," I said to Sarah.

"Mmm," she said. "It takes balls."

24

To Kiss or Not to Kiss

As far as religion is concerned, I think it's fine to believe anything you want to, as long as no one gets hurt. I try to do a minimum of harm—to other people, to the earth, to myself—and to do some good whenever possible. I figure that if you attempt to live with passion and kindness, and read a lot, you'll probably do all right. That's it for my religious manifesto.

You can't help thinking about religion, and the rituals and expectations that go along with it, when you photograph a lot of weddings. That's why I gave you my theory, by the way, because it's Monday and I shot two weddings over the weekend, and mostly because Sarah was busy this morning and couldn't meet me for our usual Monday-morning coffee-and-talking-nonsense hour. Monday-morning coffee by myself makes me philosophical. Here's the thing: Weddings can be pagan celebrations, legal proceedings, religious rituals, social production numbers, theatrical performances, or a combination of the above. What's for show, what's real, and how you decide what you really need and what's required of you by others is a complicated business. The ways different couples figure it out can lead to all sorts of compromises and confusion. This past weekend's weddings were prime examples.

*M*ary and Tom were as straight, pleasant, and normal a couple as their names implied. They were coming from Montana to be married by the ocean in Northern California. Mary and I talked briefly on the telephone, and I liked her immediately. She and Tom were clearly operating on a tight budget, and I agreed they could hire me for just a couple of hours. I could tell that coming so far to get married was a big deal for them. Mary said she wanted to honor the fact that Tom, who had grown up in the Central Valley, had spent time at this particular beach as a child with his grandfather. His grandfather had died a few months before, and having the ceremony at this same beach obviously meant a lot to him. Having the wedding in California would also allow Tom's family to attend. The ceremony would take place on a cliff near the ocean, and then everyone would go to the local Rotary Club hall to celebrate.

*M*ary called again a couple of days before they were due to drive to California.

"I just wanted to check in with you about a few things," she said. "My dad is performing the ceremony. Did I tell you that?"

"No, but how nice for you."

"Yes. And he's just about the sweetest man you'll ever

meet. It's really different for him that we're getting married at the beach and not at his church, but he's been great about it."

"His church? He's a minister, then? Or do you mean the church he goes to?"

"Oh, no, he's a minister. And there are some things you should probably know. Like, we won't be having a ring or anything."

"No wedding ring, you mean?"

"My parents don't believe in jewelry."

"Oh, OK. Anything else?"

"Well, probably we won't kiss, either, but I'm not sure about that. No, I'm pretty sure. We won't kiss. My parents wouldn't be comfortable with us kissing."

I wanted to ask her if she minded about the ring, or the kiss. She sounded a little sad. But it was none of my business, and I barely knew her. I wasn't sure at all what sort of religion would frown on wedding rings. I decided to ask a general question.

"Anything else I should know, things that might be a little, um, different?"

"Well, there definitely won't be any music at the reception. My parents don't believe in music. That sort of music, I mean. So definitely no dancing."

Mary didn't seem to think there was anything more; just no ring, no kissing, no music, and definitely no dancing. So we sorted out what time and where we would meet and said good-bye. I was a bit worried. I wanted to ask her what I should wear to the wedding. Not that I usually show up in a hoochy mama dress or anything, but I have been know to go as far as a pair of earrings. I was also a little concerned for Mary and Tom. Did they mind having these restrictions on their wedding? I needn't have worried. They had worked everything out.

*C*ontrary to my ridiculous speculations, Mary's family did not show up dressed all in black with no zippers on their clothing and driving a horse and buggy. Mary's father did not have a long white beard. And nobody thumped any Bibles or threatened fire and brimstone. Mary's father was indeed a sweet man. In fact, both her parents were lovely. They were mild, kind, and very happy for their daughter. The ceremony was short and simple. There were no rings, and there was no kissing. After hugs and handshakes all around, the guests left for the hall, and Mary told her father that she and Tom would do a few quick pictures and meet them there. She asked me if I knew a secluded spot. I took them down a steep, narrow path to a very private cove I had scouted out for previous weddings.

"Could you just watch and take some pictures?" Mary asked me. She and Tom walked about ten feet away and stood facing each other. Tom took something out of his pocket and dropped down on one knee. He took Mary's hand and said, "Mary, will you marry me?" He slipped a diamond ring on her finger, rose, and kissed her. Several times. Then from his other pocket he took a second ring. Mary took the engagement ring off her finger, and Tom slid the plain gold band on and told her he loved her. She put her engagement ring back on. They kissed some more. I took lots of pictures. Close-ups of their hands with Mary's rings showing, Mary and Tom kissing at the edge of the ocean, and Tom holding Mary in his arms and spinning around.

Finally, they decided we had done enough. Mary carefully took off her rings and gave them back to Tom. He put them in a small box and slipped it in his pocket. We shook hands, and they left for the reception. They looked very happy. Probably Mary had had some practice walking the fine line of maintaining parental respect versus satisfying personal desire. On this day, she had found a graceful answer to navigating her way through.

That was Saturday.

Sunday's wedding was another story. I had always thought it was pretty much a given that unless physical difficulties made it impossible, the wedding ceremony ended with a kiss. Mary and Tom had shown me a new variation on that theory on Saturday. On Sunday, I was to be proven wrong again. Twice in a weekend—just shows you what I know.

*P*aul and Rachel had decided to have their portraits taken just before the ceremony. Blessed with a glorious October day in Napa, they couldn't have chosen a lovelier place for their pictures. The grapevines were turning deep shades of red and gold, and the sunlight was filtered gently by just enough cloud to hide a few rough edges and make everyone look good. With Sarah maneuvering the bride's long veil past the treacherous bits of trailing vine, we headed out into the vineyard directly behind the restaurant where the ceremony was to take place. A few guests who had arrived early stood on the back patio sipping mimosas and watching us.

The vineyards looked lovely with the vines laid out in neat rows stretching away to the hills in the distance. I found a good spot for Paul and Rachel to stand. Usually I just leave the bride and groom alone to talk to each other and move quietly around them, watching what happens while they have a few minutes to themselves. It's a pleasure to watch the couple forget about me. Forget about how they look. Forget about smiling for the camera. I want them to just relax. Once they stop worrying about anything, I can photograph them talking, laughing, or just being peaceful before the rush of the ceremony and party begins. Sarah stays well back and moves in quietly now and again if the veil catches on a vine or if I need something.

Rachel and Paul were happy to oblige. They stood between two long rows of vines chatting easily. After a few minutes I noticed a change in their posture. Rachel had pulled away from Paul and was shaking her head. Paul appeared to be making a point. Emphatically. Then they began to argue in earnest. It's very hard to take romantic portraits of a couple who are having a heated argument. It's also embarrassing. I must admit, though, I was curious. What on earth could they be having a huge argument about on their wedding day when everything had seemed idyllic just a couple of moments before?

"Hey. Sarah, go over there and adjust her veil, would you?"

Sarah laughed at me.

"You're kidding, right?"

"What?"

"You just want me to go over there and spy on them for

you. No way. Do your own eavesdropping. I'm not getting in the middle of that."

She had a point. Things appeared to be escalating. There were raised voices and Rachel looked like she was crying. That's very bad for wedding pictures—unless the tears are are tears of joy, of course, which these obviously were not.

"It's a mess," said Sarah grimly. She was right. I decided I'd better try to move in a bit closer and find out what was going on.

"I don't think it's a good idea, that's all," Rachel was saying.

Paul scowled. "Why not? We don't have to do a big one or anything, and it's just one time."

"But why do we have to? You know I don't like it. Why make such a big deal about it."

"Fine, if you hate it that much then we won't." Paul started to walk away. Rachel grabbed his arm.

"I didn't say I hated it," she said, now crying in earnest. "I'd just feel more comfortable."

"Great. Let's just make sure you're comfortable, then. We certainly won't worry about what our guests feel or think. We won't care if we disappoint everybody."

I got a few pictures from behind as they both stalked back to the restaurant. From that angle you couldn't see that their faces were stony. They looked quite nice. Sarah and I stood around for a bit, speculating about the cause of the blowup and keeping our distance from the warring couple, then wandered back inside ourselves. Figuring I'd better try to find out what was up, I went looking for the maid of honor to see if she could help. I had met her earlier in the day. She was a cousin of the bride, in possession of a set of brand-new twin girls. She seemed to have a good sense of humor—a definite asset when you are a maid of honor or the mother of newborn twins. I finally found her in the restaurant kitchen mixing up formula with one hand and burping a baby with the other.

"The bride and groom seemed a little upset when we were doing the pictures. Everything OK?"

She shrugged, which made the baby burp. She kissed his nose. "I know it's hard to believe, but the problem is the kiss."

"The kiss?" I didn't see how the kiss could be a problem. It's usually one of the few moments in a wedding that you can count on to be trouble-free. It pretty much takes care of itself, right? I mean, barring serious dental issues or the kind of inappropriate performance that caused a guest at one wedding I photographed to shout, "Get a room," even though we were in a church.

"She doesn't want to," said the maid of honor.

"She doesn't want to kiss?" This was a new one. I couldn't wait to tell Sarah.

"No. She doesn't like kissing much anyway, but it makes her especially uncomfortable in public. Paul told her that she's going to disappoint all the guests and ruin the whole wedding. He said that the guests expect a kiss and if they don't see one they'll feel cheated. He's worried about what everyone will think."

If I were Paul, I'd be a lot more worried about the fact that my future bride didn't like to kiss. "Oh, dear." I couldn't think of anything else to say. This was too weird.

"Exactly." Both babies were now crying. "Listen, I've got to feed these two and try to get them to sleep. After that I'll go see what I can do." She headed out of the kitchen with a howling baby on each shoulder. I figured she might not be able to help very soon.

Sarah came in. I'd sent her to find Paul and Rachel and see if they might be ready to finish doing their portraits. Judging from what I had just heard and from the look on Sarah's face, it didn't seem likely.

"Forget it," said Sarah. "Not gonna happen. She's in tears and he's pissed."

$\mathcal{D}$uring the ceremony, Rachel looked tremulous and Paul angry. At the end she hugged him and he relented just enough to hug her back. Barely. The guests cheered and politely ignored the tension. The whole thing felt ridiculous. Like an exercise in spoiling your own fun. Paul was more concerned about his guests than about his bride, and Rachel couldn't break through her inhibitions enough to give him one public kiss when it really mattered. It seemed a poor start to a marriage. And you had to wonder—I mean, if you were the kind of person who wondered about that sort of thing—how Rachel felt about the other kinds of physical contact that are part of marriage. Of course, Sarah and I never speculated about that sort of thing. Well, maybe once in a while.

25

Why Teaching Matters

At first, our move to San Francisco seemed to be just the change we needed, but a year into our new life, things weren't going so well. John and I were arguing, which in itself was unusual. Worse, we were arguing about the sorts of things we had sworn would never upset us. Things we didn't even care about. Who had forgotten to put the wash in the dryer. Parking tickets. What to have for dinner. He left for work in the morning before I got up. We were communicating by e-mail, something we had said we wouldn't be caught dead doing. When he came home, I didn't want to hear about his day spent writing marketing hype for techno-geek software, and he was in no mood to sympathize with my complaints about yet another day spent in the excitement of the sandbox at the local playground, my efforts to find the perfect sippy cup at the drugstore, or the lack of a great Play-Doh recipe online.

I don't know who was more bored. The only thing that seemed certain was that we had gone off the rails somewhere.

But knowing that things aren't working the way they should be doesn't mean you know how to fix the problem. It took quite a while, after our move to San Francisco, to understand what was not right with the way we were living. The way we lived now was so many other people's idea of happiness. We figured there must be something wrong with us. We plugged away at being happy.

Still, the balance was off. And when John came to me and told me that his long days in the world of marketing were making him miserable, it was hardly a surprise. By now it was clear that this newfound security we had acquired along with a bigger paycheck had a price of its own. One we were not willing to pay. He was no more suited to the work he was doing than I was to channeling all my creative energy into art projects for a toddler. I missed my work. Even our daughter looked fed up by the end of the day. My husband said that he'd been thinking. What he really wanted to do was to teach, because teaching mattered. It was good, interesting, and worthwhile work. He wanted to teach high school kids about literature and creative writing and to introduce them to the books and ideas that he loved. Also, he wanted me to stay awake once in a while when he talked about what he did. Of course, because teaching mattered, it would pay him a salary that was about one-quarter of what he made now.

For most of my adult life I have had the privilege of choosing to do work that I love doing. Because of that choice, I have lived alone and loved men who required no commitment. I have traveled a great deal, sometimes been discouraged, and often been unable to pay the rent. I've had migraines and nightmares and more funny, fascinating, and truly perfect days than I could possibly count. And I have always felt marvelously free. Now, since I had fallen in love, married, and had a child, the roof needed to be kept over three people's heads, not just my own.

I decided I would start photographing weddings again. But this time, it would be different, because life was different for me now. Photographing weddings would no longer be something I was doing to keep body and soul together while my world was coming apart. I could photograph them on my own terms, and find a way of seeing and reflecting weddings that was true. I would tell my clients that what I wanted to do was tell the story of their day as it actually unfolded. Not a glossed-over, stock version of a wedding that left them with images that were interchangeable with those in a hundred other wedding albums, but pictures that might, twenty years from now, actually remind them of what they were feeling on their wedding day.

This suddenly felt like something wonderful. A chance to be accorded extraordinary access to the lives and emotions of people on a day that was truly important to them—an opportunity to intimately document a high point in a couple's life. It was a privilege, and a fascinating one at that. And I would be doing my share to support my family. Deciding to photograph weddings again felt just fine.

And that is how we live now. My husband teaches high school students about writing well and loving books, and I photograph weddings—and lots of other things that don't help to pay the rent at all. The dinner table talk is terrific, and in the summer the three of us have so much time to-gether we almost get enough of each other. Sometimes, when I have had a hard night, or he has forty ninth-grade essays on *Heart of Darkness* to grade on a sunny Saturday, we wonder if this is really what we wanted. But that thought never lasts long, because we both know that the life we are lucky enough to be leading is exactly the one we chose.

26

The Ugly Bride,
or
Pretty Is as Pretty Does

$\mathcal{I}$t is a truth universally ignored that not all babies are cute and not all brides are lovely. I have photographed a lot of babies and a lot of brides, and I stand witness to the fact that some are definitely ugly. Others are just plain hideous. They are bald, they drool, and their ears stick out. Their noses run nasty green stuff, and they get stinky and have dermatitis and no eyebrows. The babies, I mean. The brides are another matter. How pretty a bride is has very little to do with looks.

$\mathcal{S}$he's ugly," said Sarah.

The bride Sarah was looking at was in fact one of the loveliest I'd ever seen: tall, toned to just the right degree of firmness, with dewy skin, green eyes, and tousled blond hair that it had only taken the stylist an hour to whip into perfect just-out-of-bed disarray. Her pouty lips looked like she had come by them naturally. Her features were so symmetrical that she was, well, as far as I was concerned, of no interest at all. But she was certainly lovely. Right down to her French-manicured fingertips that she was tapping impatiently on the arm of her chair. Monica wanted a drink.

"She's ugly, and she's decided she's making a mistake," said Sarah. "People don't drink that much before their wedding unless they think they're making a mistake."

It's true. Monica did appear to be having a classic case of buyer's remorse. She certainly didn't look excited or happy. She looked aggravated and a little bored.

"Have you seen it out there?" I asked Sarah. "Thousands of orchids flown in from Hawaii, bone china and crystal place settings for four hundred. One of those massive ice sculptures you pour the martinis down to chill them. There's a thirteen-man band setting up."

"Bad time to change your mind."

"The worst."

I didn't think Monica was going to change her mind, though. She'd made her decision long before, probably when she and her sorority sisters had been evaluating various suitors for their ability to keep them in the style they required. Harris had looked like the best prospect. His pedigree was excellent. He'd been an undergrad at the same Ivy League school her brother went to, and now he was almost finished with his MBA and had a spot waiting for him at his father's brokerage firm. His family had a place in Vail to go skiing and a house on Nantucket that they always went to for the summers. The diamond on her finger was the size of a marble. Monica was sticking to the plan. She might be regretting that she had decided to marry a dull and arrogant man for the sake of money, but that was nothing that seven shots of chilled Stoli in a silver shot glass wouldn't cure.

Monica's mother arrived bearing a tray, and Monica's fingers stopped tapping.

"Where did you have to go for it, Russia?" said Monica, and downed the shot.

Monica's mother wasn't bothered by her daughter's rudeness. She was busy making sure her daughter married well, just as she had herself. And Harris's family was everything Monica's mother wanted; in fact, the business connection was also an excellent one for her husband. This wedding would happen, even if she had to deliver the whole bottle of vodka to her daughter to make sure it did.

"Ugly," said Sarah. "Can we get out of here for a while?"

"Let's go find Harris," I said.

*H*arris and his groomsmen were getting ready in the guest cottage on the grounds of Monica's parents' estate. The cottage had six bedrooms and a grand piano. When Sarah and I walked in, one of the groomsmen was playing the piano wearing nothing but red, white, and blue boxers. The others were sprawled around the room on couches and easy chairs watching a football game with the sound turned off and laughing at the medley of songs the groomsman was playing.

Harris was having an IV line inserted into his arm by one of the groomsmen.

"She's a rich girl . . ." Harris sang along happily, apparently unconcerned by the medical procedure taking place.

Sarah and I exchanged glances.

"Are you ill?" To me, an IV line meant something serious must be wrong, but Harris just laughed.

"I'm fine. James is a medical student," he said, indicating the man who was now hanging a bag of fluid on a portable IV stand. "He's just helping me out."

"A hangover is nothing but dehydration," James said. "You just pump some fluids back in and you're good to go. I'm fixing up our boy here."

"Gotta use the head," said Harris. He went off in the direction of the bathroom, rolling the IV stand alongside.

"This isn't exactly pretty, either," I said to Sarah.

"Match made in heaven."

While Monica was busy trying to get enough liquor into her system and Harris was washing too much of it out of his, Sarah and I went to check out the preparations. Under the white silk canopy the size of a circus tent, it looked like a flower show. There were pink and white orchids everywhere. They garlanded the tent poles, spilled from huge urns at the corners of the dance floor, and were elaborately arranged in vases in the center of each table. The white-gloved catering staff was putting the finishing touches on an elaborate display of caviar and Russian vodkas. Dozens of bottles of Cristal were chilling in ice-filled tubs. The catering manager rushed past and then stopped midflight to turn back to us.

"Are you two the photographers?" she asked. "Well, there's some food set up for you downstairs, but you'd better hurry up before it's all gone. The band just went down there, and there are an awful lot of them." She dashed off.

We wandered down into the bowels of the house, getting lost and stopping to ask for directions several times along the way. Finally, we found what appeared to be a laundry room where a large folding table had been set up with chairs around it. On the table were some packages of bologna and sliced cheese, several loaves of Wonder Bread, a bowl of tomatoes, a squeeze bottle of mustard, and some three-liter bottles of Pepsi. There were paper plates and a package of plastic knives. The band members were standing around the table looking unhappy.

"Did you see that mountain of lobster salad upstairs?" asked one. "Are they kidding here, or what?"

No one had an answer.

"Man," said a huge guy in dark glasses and dreadlocks who appeared to be the bandleader, "these folks are screwed up. Haven't they heard that one about not biting the hand that feeds you? 'Cause they ain't feedin' us right, and now I'm getting a serious urge to bite someone. They just broke rule number one: Feed your band."

"And your photographers," I added.

"Anyone got a cell phone?" Sarah said. "We could order pizza. I know a great place near here."

The bandleader put a huge arm around Sarah.

"Now, that's good thinking. Tell you what," he said, "you order the pizzas, and I'll just tack it on to the bill we'll be handing these folks at the end of the night. I'd like to see them argue with me about it." He looked fierce. "And Billy," he called over to a guy who was pouring himself a soda, "stop messing with that crap and see if you can go score us something real to drink from upstairs. Try the guy at the back bar. Tell him Big Ray from Oakland says hello."

Everyone started looking a lot happier. Sarah ordered pizza. Billy came back with four bottles of red wine and some glasses. By the time we all had to get back to work we were feeling pretty good, and Sarah had a date to meet Big Ray at a club in Oakland the following weekend.

*U*pstairs, things were no more fun than they had been before. Monica looked flawlessly lovely, and we went out into the manicured grounds and did portraits of her holding her flowers at just the right angle, with her head tilted slightly to best show off her graceful neck. Her bridesmaids spread out her train behind her and meticulously arranged each fold. Monica looked like she wished she was somewhere else but smiled perfectly for each photograph. The smile faded a moment after each picture. There was no hint of animation to liven things up. Not even a breeze dared fluff up her pre-fluffed hair. Her mother told her to smile and tried to rearrange her veil, but Monica slapped her hand away.

"Leave it, Mother," she snapped. "I know what I'm doing." She turned to her bridesmaids. "How do I look?"

"Perfect," said one bridesmaid.

"Just like a contessa," said her maid of honor.

Monica looked satisfied.

She turned to me. "Do you have everything you need?"

I told her we did. There was no point in doing anything more. Monica was the idea of a bride, perfectly executed— and as dull to photograph as any bride I had ever shot.

"There goes most wedding photographers' idea of the ideal subject," I said as Sarah and I watched the women walk back toward the house.

"If you like dead things," Sarah said.

"She's beautiful, though, right?" Sarah just shrugged. Like me, Sarah is partial to beauty that is rooted in something other than a perfect face and body.

"Harris's turn," I reminded her.

*B*arris had disconnected himself from his IV and had put on a seersucker suit and a pink silk bow tie. His groomsmen were also in seersucker, but their ties were pale blue. Visually they were quite striking.

"Wow," said Sarah. "That's a serious amount of stripes."

"Let's look for a nice quiet background," I suggested.

The groom had something else in mind.

"We're going to do pictures over here," he said. He walked off in the direction of a lawn bordered with flowers.

Sarah raised her eyebrows at me. She knows that I'm not partial to being told what we are or are not going to do.

"Twerp," I said—and went over to where he was waiting.

"Get this shot," ordered Harris. "We're going to do some of those flying pictures. You ready?"

His groomsmen lined up in two rows in front of him and put out their arms to make a sort of sling, and then Harris launched himself through the air with his arms extended in front of him like Superman.

"Here I come to save the day," he sang.

He flew, briefly, and then crashed through his groomsmen's arms and onto the grass. They all pig-piled on top of him and started laughing hysterically.

"I don't think he got all the alcohol out," I said to Sarah.

"No kidding."

When Harris finally emerged from under the heap of groomsmen, he looked a mess. There were grass stains on the knees of his seersucker suit, his bow tie was sideways, and his dainty little boutonniere was missing entirely.

"Well, I believe we're finished here, gentlemen. Back to the shack for a cocktail, I think," said Harris. He walked away.

"Come on, men, we better go clean our boy up. These ladies will just have to catch us later. Right, ladies?" said the best man. He and the groomsmen headed off after Harris.

"Guess we'll try for some more pictures later, right, lady?" said Sarah.

"What? You don't think the flying seersucker Superman shot is going to do it for Monica's mummy? You know, I think I've had just about enough of this ice bride and her arrogant husband-to-be."

"We could go see what the band's doing," Sarah said hopefully.

"Later. We've still got a wedding to shoot."

And shoot it we did. For hours. Through it all, Monica and Harris barely spoke to each other except when it was necessary for the completion of some part of the ritual. Monica continued to snap at her mother, spend most of her time with her bridesmaids and sorority sisters, and look lovely. Harris spent almost all of the evening with his groomsmen, exchanging stories from their undergraduate days, drinking Chivas, and smoking Cuban cigars.

At the end of the evening, I spoke briefly with Monica.

She looked just as fresh as she had at the beginning of the wedding. She was all business.

"We're leaving for Nevis tomorrow morning. We'll be back in a couple of weeks, but it's best if you just send the pictures here to my mother. She'll know what to do with them. How do you think you did? I hope the pictures will be good."

"I think your pictures will be lovely. It was a very pretty wedding."

"Yes." She looked pleased. "Everything looked just right, didn't it? I wanted it to look perfect."

$\mathcal{T}$hree years later, when I photographed Monica's sister's wedding, everything looked just right all over again. Monica and Harris were not there. They had divorced after eighteen months, and Monica had chosen not to attend.

27

Romance

$\mathcal{I}$t's one thing if religion or personal inhibitions prevent you from getting married exactly as you might wish. It's quite another when everyone around you offers advice and tells you that what you want is all wrong. Poor Shoshonna was struggling to keep her ideas about her wedding intact in the face of too much good advice.

"My mother says I'll look like an idiot," she said the first time I met her.

Shoshonna was a small bulldog of a person. Solid, stocky, and determined. She had a round, pleasant face, brown hair worn neatly trimmed at shoulder length, and an apparent fondness for big baggy sweatshirts. The one she was wearing as she sat on my couch biting her nails and looking worried said GO GIANTS. She looked a little frumpy and very practical. But inside Shoshonna lurked another person altogether. As sometimes happens in the process of wedding planning, Shoshonna's inner romantic had been set free. It must have been trapped in there for quite a while, because it was sure going nuts now.

"I wanted to look like Guinevere," said Shoshonna. "I wanted long, flowing hair extensions, and one of those filmy dresses with the big dangly sleeves and a wreath of spring flowers in my hair." Her eyes were shining. She looked lovely.

"Did you ever see *Camelot,* Claire? I mean the movie?" I had. In fact, I had just watched it again recently with my daughter.

"You know that scene where Vanessa Redgrave goes out to pick flowers on May Day? That's how I wanted to feel."

I knew just what she meant. "Who wouldn't want to feel that way?"

She gave me a huge smile. "Our friend Maya was going to play guitar. She knows lots of old folk tunes." She grinned. "A little vintage Joni Mitchell, some—" She paused. "Do you think I'm nuts?"

"Why would I?"

"I'm not exactly anyone's idea of the Renaissance maiden type, am I? That's what my mother said. It's what my new mother-in-law said, too. They want us to get married at the Hyatt. In the ballroom. I'm supposed to go dress shopping with them both next week."

"Are you going to go?" I was curious. Shoshonna looked unhappy, but she didn't look like a pushover.

She was quiet for a minute. "No," she said. "I do know I may end up looking like some crazy person at a Renaissance fair, but I've always wanted it this way. So does Sam. We both just want to get married barefoot in an old apple orchard and with no one worrying about anything. Sam found this great white shirt with big billowy sleeves and a thing at the neck that laces up with a leather cord. He looks fantastic in it. My mom doesn't know, but we're having Celtic wedding rings designed. I don't know why everyone else is hassling us about getting married the way we want. It's our wedding, and that's the way it's going to be. I think."

That last little "I think" worried me. Shoshonna still had a few battles ahead of her. I wondered how it would turn out. Listening to her, I thought about all the times I'd heard people tell me their wedding plans. Plans full of angst and compromises and family tension. Or crazy plans that were way off the mark of what would have been easy or fun. Many times it just seemed to be all about the show they would be presenting to the outside world. But this was completely different. Shoshonna knew exactly what she wanted, and for all the right reasons.

"I think you should just go for it," I told her, even though it was none of my business. It's hard not to get involved sometimes. "You'll both look fantastic, and I'll take the pictures to prove it. And no matter what, you'll have the wedding you really wanted. That happens a lot less often than you might think."

"We'll see," she said. She looked pretty determined.

Eight months later, Sam and Shoshonna got married in a beautiful old apple orchard. Shoshonna walked barefoot across the lawn carrying sunflowers. There were bright ribbons braided into her hair extensions. She wore a pale green gown with long flowing sleeves that made her feel like

Guinevere, and Sam kissed her the minute she arrived at his side. And later, while a reggae band played and guests sneaked off to find hiding places in the tall grass where they could make out and smoke pot, Shoshonna's mother danced barefoot to Bob Marley. So sometimes the visions work out, especially when it's about happiness and not about making a show. Then the pleasure of the couple becomes contagious, and everyone—even the most critical parent or friend—gets swept up into the romance.

*O*ne of the best examples of sheer enthusiasm sweeping a wedding along was the celebration of the marriage of Sade and Lola. Both former members of a dance company, they were now busy opening what they were determined would be the premier gym in San Francisco. We met to walk through the wedding site they had chosen. It was a venerable old San Francisco club filled with art deco touches. It had an atmosphere somewhere between a high-class bordello, a speakeasy, and Rick's Café in *Casablanca*. No one was telling Sade and Lola how to do anything, and they knew exactly what they wanted.

"Here's the plan!" said Sade. Everything Sade said sounded like it had an exclamation point on the end. He was the most relentlessly enthusiastic and constantly mobile person I had ever met. I wish I could explain to you why he was not a jerk. He should have been. He had all the makings of being one, but instead, he was charming.

Lola moved more slowly, with the studied grace of a dancer. She watched Sade and smiled, slowing him down with barely a word or two if his enthusiasm started getting out of hand. She treated him one moment as a lover, and the next as a crazy younger brother she was keeping an eye on. But she never said a word against any of his ideas. And Sade had a lot of ideas.

"You'll be the paparazzi, Claire. The place will be like a 1920s nightclub. Smoky, with a sax player in the corner. You're there to catch it all in black-and-white. The romance. The drama. A little bad behavior. Lola looking sultry and beautiful. Me in my suit. I'm having a white suit made. It's a copy of one Bogart wore. And martinis! The most amazing martini bar you ever saw. We'll have a martini menu with hundreds of choices."

"About twenty choices," murmured Lola.

Sade kissed her, then asked me, "Do you like martinis, Claire?"

"Sure." I've been known to have a martini or two.

"Well, you'll love these."

"Sade wants everyone to be as happy as possible." Lola laughed.

Sade grabbed her hand.

"Want to see our first dance?"

He swept her off into the middle of the room. They stood facing each other. Very slowly Sade slipped out of his leather jacket and, without looking, tossed it over his shoulder to me. Like an attentive stagehand, or perhaps an extra in Sade's movie, I made a dive for it and caught it just before it hit the floor. I was rather pleased with myself. For the next few minutes I watched Sade and Lola tango and swoop their way blissfully around the room as they danced to the music in their heads. They ended in a perfect dip, held it for a moment, and walked back over to me.

"See? Martinis, white suit, paparazzi. It all makes perfect sense." He was perfectly right.

28

House Rules

$\mathcal{I}$'ve had studios and storefront spaces of my own and have designed, built, and spent countless hours in five different darkrooms. These days, my husband, daughter, and I live in the second most expensive city in America, and we love it. So, for reasons both economic and practical, I work from home. When you live in a relatively small space that doubles as both your office and your home, it's important to be clear about the house rules.

Our home is where clients come to look at my portfolios, decide if I'm the right person for the job, and, later, pick up their finished work. So the place needs to be pretty clean and tidy most of the time. We're all supposed to pick up after ourselves. With a busy life and a very busy young daughter, we often lose the battle for cleanliness and order. Even if, at the last minute, I do manage to shove the toys under the couch, dig the modeling clay out of the rug, burn scented candles to cover the smell coming from the guinea pig's cage, and remember to sweep up the amazing amount of sand that fell out of those little sneakers and trailed its way up the stairs, this will be the time the client will ask to use the bathroom and my daughter will have started a new science experiment in the sink.

Once in a while, things seem to be running smoothly. My home is clean and odor-free. John is somewhere in the back half of the apartment making sure that our daughter will not drown in the bath. I have bought flowers and lit candles and am showing my portfolio to a bride. That's when the door from the kitchen crashes open and my daughter flies through. She is in her Spider-Man pajamas, soaking wet, and clutching something in her hands. It's clear that the rule that you are not supposed to disturb Mummy when she's having a meeting is about to be broken.

"Mum," she says, "Dad says I can't wash Sly's hair in the tub, but I can, can't I?"

At this point a bewildered, slightly squashed, and very wet guinea pig is deposited on my open portfolio that has no plastic pages covering the beautiful archival prints I spent hours working on. Little wet footprints blossom all over the page.

"I hate rats," the bride says.

"Oh, Sly's not a rat," says my daughter. She is seven years old, plans to be a veterinarian, and loves teaching people about animals. "Rats and guinea pigs are quite different, really. For one thing, guinea pigs' tails aren't long, and they don't live in the wild anymore, either. Well, they do in Peru, but we don't talk about that because they eat guinea pigs in Peru and I'm a vegetarian. I want to be a vegan, but it's hard."

"Can you please just catch it?" asks my client. She's off the couch and halfway to the door.

My daughter tries to catch her guinea pig while I try to catch my client, who is headed down the stairs. My husband is nowhere in sight. He's usually quite brave, but I suspect he's hiding somewhere.

"Mum, Sly's behind the couch. I need help. Don't squash him. Be careful. He's scared. There he goes. Get him!" My daughter is laughing. I hear the front door slam shut.

*S*ome time later, Sly is back in his cage, having narrowly escaped a shampoo and blow-dry. We are all in the kitchen eating leftovers, and my daughter tells me that "no one, no one, Mum, could really think a guinea pig was a rat!"

"Sweetie, you have to respect Mum's work, you know," I tell her.

It's probably time for a serious talk about appropriate behavior. Perhaps a review of the rules of the house? Still, it's true that a guinea pig doesn't look anything like a rat, and anyway, who wants a client who can't recognize something funny when it jumps right into her lap? And, in general, my daughter understands the rules of our jumbled-up life. Don't answer the phone during business hours or you might have to talk to one of Mum's crazy clients. Don't step on, color on, or in any way distress the pictures that are sometimes spread out all over the floor. No means no, so no arguing or whining. That last rule seems pretty straightforward to me, and to my daughter. Not so my clients.

*W*hat is it about saying no to brides? If I say no to Sarah, something I don't risk doing very often, she may argue or get pissed, but she certainly knows what I mean. As in, "No,

Sarah, don't get drinks from the bar before the guests have had a chance even if it does mean you get yours first that way." Or, "No, Sarah, I don't think it is OK for us to tell the bride's mother the truth when she asks you if her dress makes her look fat." That sort of thing. But a surprising number of my brides hear no and decide it means yes. The more I say, "No, I am not the right person to photograph your wedding," the more they decide that I am in fact the only one to do so.

Heather from Los Angeles was one of those brides. She called to get more information about my services. Unfortunately, we established that I was not yet booked for her wedding date before we really started talking. This eliminated the best answer to situations like this one: simply saying how sorry I was to be already booked.

"I've heard all about your work, and I loved your Web site."

"Thanks."

"I really need someone who works digitally."

"Oh, well, that's too bad. I'm afraid I only shoot film."

"Well, I've done a lot of research that supports the fact that digital images make better enlargements, so I'm really sure that's the way I need to go."

"Well, perhaps I'm not the photographer for you then, right? But thanks for calling."

"Wait! That's really my decision, isn't it?"

"I see it as more of a two-way situation. After all, I'd hate to disappoint you, and you say you want digital photography. So now we both know that I'm the wrong person for you. But I appreciate you giving me a call."

"Aren't you going to tell me why film would be better?"

"No."

"So you don't want to shoot my wedding?" Heather sounded petulant. Not a tone likely to bring out my warm and sympathetic side.

"Tell you what, why don't you tell me a bit about the style of photography you're looking for."

"I'm not at all into that documentary stuff. You know what I mean, that candid stuff with no retouching and people looking like they have no idea the camera is even there or they forgot to put on their makeup. Like those PBS documentaries. Plus, I saw lots of black-and-white on your Web site, and I was thinking that the great thing about digital would be that you could shoot all the pictures in black-and-white in your head if that's what you like better, but I could get them printed in color because I like that better. That would be perfect for both of us."

"Except that I don't shoot digitally."

"I know. That's why I feel so disappointed."

I didn't feel inclined to help her out about that feeling. Teaching her to deal with disappointment seemed to me something her mummy or daddy should have done about twenty years ago.

"Did you notice the style of my work at all? It's definitely more the kind of thing that you're saying you don't like."

"But you work in the style the customer wants, right? I mean, they're the ones hiring you—and paying you. Your job is to please the customer."

"I'm sorry. I have another call coming in that I really have to take. I just don't think that I'm the right person for you at all, I want to wish you the best of luck finding—"

"I'll just look over your pricing information and stuff and get back to you. Bye."

OK, so I don't have call waiting. But she was really bugging me. Two days later, she sent me an e-mail.

Claire,

I enjoyed our conversation. I really don't understand why you don't shoot digitally. It would be cheaper for you, as well as better for your clients. I did look at your site again, and I do see that you definitely shoot in a documentary style. Which is still not my favorite. Could you please send me a copy of your contract?

I wrote back telling her that I was absolutely not the person for her. I told her that I felt she would be disappointed by my work and that I would feel bad about agreeing to photograph her wedding since I would not be able to shoot for her in the way she wanted. I did not attach a contract. She wrote back right away.

Hi Claire,

Thanks for your e-mail! You forgot to attach the contract!

I sent one. Just to see what would happen. She sent it back by overnight FedEx, signed and with a deposit check. And I was stuck.

Which brings me to one of the other, and most important, rules of our home: When Mum gets that look on her face and starts muttering about how she never wants to shoot another wedding ever again, it's best to find Dad and suggest you both take Mum out to dinner. If you sit somewhere nice, buy her a glass of wine, talk about other things, and plan what you'll do together next weekend when, you remind her, she is not booked to shoot a wedding, she cheers up. Then, when she gets home, you can help her draw a little skull and crossbones on the contract of the crazy bride and bury it deep in next year's files. By then, you tell her, maybe she can think of a way to convince Sarah to do it.

29

The Butterfly and the Bulldozer

$\mathcal{I}$ like the title of this chapter, so I'm sticking with it—even though, technically, it's not entirely accurate. The thing is, although Shelby had some of the qualities of a fragile insect with a short lifespan, there was a nice little bit of pit bull mixed in, too. And as for Antoine, well, if he did crush lots of people underfoot, it was done with such joie de vivre that after a while they stopped minding and just let themselves get squashed. Still, I stand by my title. The winner of this battle was a foregone conclusion from the get-go.

$\mathcal{I}$ arrived at the huge downtown hotel at the same time as the bride and groom. Ann and Paul were nice people. Both were in the last year of an MBA program at Stanford. They were clever, low-maintenance, and very busy. They wanted a fairly straightforward day: Get dressed at a pretty hotel, take some photographs at a good location, have a short wedding ceremony, and finish with a great party. There were only 150 guests coming. No children. And the ceremony and reception were all to take place here at the hotel. This one would be a breeze for the coordinator. Or so you would have thought. But this was not just any coordinator, this was Shelby. And for Shelby, it was to be her flagship event, the one that would put her fledgling wedding planner business on the map. She had recently left corporate event planning to start her own company, and this was only her second solo event. She was nervous and determined, and she'd done a lot of reading about how to be successful in business. No detail was going to be left to chance.

The front desk attendant directed us to the ballroom. Pushing open the heavy double doors, we stepped into a vast and empty space. In the very middle was one round table, elaborately decked out for a party. It looked a bit forlorn there all alone in the middle of the room, as though the party had moved on elsewhere and left it behind.

"Sit, sit," shouted Shelby, waving us over. "We're just waiting for Antoine." She was busy rustling and rearranging something in front of her on the table. "Come and look at the flowers and the table settings. I've got it all set up for you." Paul, Ann, and I trekked across the open space. "Did you bring all your paperwork, everybody? Don't worry if you're missing something. I have plenty of copies of everything. Did you all get this morning's e-mail with the meeting agenda for today?"

I had. After reading point one I had deleted the whole message. Point one was *Review this meeting agenda.*

I don't usually do meetings. Oh, I'll do site visits with a bride and groom, especially when it's a new location. Having done this work for almost twenty years, I'm not easily thrown by being at an unfamiliar winery or church. But try telling some couples that. They want you to walk every inch of the property with them—preferably at the exact time you will actually be there on the big day—so as to know where the light will be best. I don't mind. On a nice sunny day, it's a pleasure to drive out of the city over the Golden Gate and up into Napa. Wandering around a winery is never a chore, and settling all the details on-site relieves some pre-wedding tension for the couple. But today was the other kind of meeting. This was the kind that happens when a wedding planner is either new to the business or obsessively organized. Shelby was both.

Her e-mails had started arriving about a month before. The first one said: *Greetings, members of Team Ann and Paul.* As far as I was concerned, this was not a good beginning. It sounded like she was going to have matching T-shirts printed up and make us learn a team cheer, and the tone was definitely too chirpy. The e-mail continued: *The countdown has begun! Only thirty-five days left till Ann and Paul's big day. I'll be keeping you all posted on the details as we move closer and closer to the event. Can't wait to meet you in person at our vendor pep rally!* Vendor pep rally? Not in my contract.

After that the updates came about twice a week. There were schedules, revised schedules, and revisions of the revisions. I was also copied on e-mails to Flowers by Susan, Cake Mania, Artful Linens, and Golden Ticket Valet Parking Service, which probably meant that all of those lovely people were aware of Ann and Paul's preferred shot list and what time I'd be eating my vendor meal. No doubt that information was as crucial to them as the exact time of the napkin delivery was to me.

I took to deleting Shelby's mail automatically, but luckily I did read the one that told me a meeting had been scheduled. A vendor summit, she called it. Team Ann and Paul was to meet at the site the week before the wedding and *iron out the details, get our final game plan set, and just plain get excited together!* Oh boy. So here we were. Or at least, Ann, Paul, and I were here, because as we made our way over to Shelby several things became clear. First, that I was the only vendor here. No florist. No bakery representative. No DJ.

"They're all so overscheduled at this time of year. Things just came up at the last minute for most of the others," said Shelby.

I'll bet they did.

"But I'll e-mail them all the details so everyone will still be in the loop." Shelby gathered up the information packets that had been laid out for vendors who would not be attending. Her cell phone rang, and after a brief conversation she snapped it shut and picked up one more of the folders. "My, everyone sure is busy, busy." She sounded put out.

The second thing we all saw was that Shelby had indeed brought copies of everything. There were stacks of papers all over the place.

"Oh, I see you haven't got anything with you?" Shelby looked at me with a worried frown. I felt sort of bad. She looked so stressed.

"I did read everything," I told her, "and I have the schedule." I could tell that the folded piece of paper I pulled out of the back pocket of my jeans was not the sort of responsible documentation Shelby had in mind. I was not being a team player.

We all got settled and waited for Antoine, the hotel's event manager, to arrive. Shelby was small, perhaps five-two, and juicy. Everything on Shelby looked curvy. She had long, smooth black hair that she wore loose and liked to flip around a lot. Strands kept getting stuck in her lip gloss, and she'd have to stop what she was saying to pull them loose and tuck the sticky hair back behind her ear. She was wearing pale gold high heels, tight black pants, and a vividly turquoise blouse that was unbuttoned enough to make you want to congratulate her on her excellently maintained cleavage. Just in case you didn't get the point, a long gold chain with a religious medal of some kind on the end dangled right where your eyes were supposed to go. Shelby had certainly shed her corporate wardrobe. When Antoine arrived moments later—bursting through the double doors with a loud "Allo" aimed at the room in general—he took one look at Shelby and smiled.

Antoine was no slouch in the fashion department himself. Every inch of him was polished to a high sheen. His shoes were shined, his glossy pale gray suit was beautifully cut, and his light blue shirt and tie with a subtle pink stripe had been carefully chosen. His dark mustache had the sleek and glossy look you see on the fur of cats who have been sitting around grooming themselves all day in the sunshine. "Ladies, ladies, what a pleasure to see three such beautiful ladies." Antoine practically bowed. He had a courtly manner and a French accent that sounded, to my ear, a little stronger than it needed to be. He turned toward me, gave me the full wattage of his white-toothed smile, and said "Ah, the lovely bride. May I congratulate you?"

"Thanks, but no. I'm just the lovely photographer," I said. I gave him my best smile back.

Antoine was not even momentarily put out. He swiveled smoothly toward Ann. "My dear, so many beauties to choose from. Lovely, so lovely." He bowed slightly toward Paul. "And sir groom, hello to you, of course." He shook Paul's hand. "But we must always greet the ladies first, eh?"

Having made his entrance, he sat down in the empty chair next to Shelby and said, "My dear, shall we begin?"

That was Shelby's cue, and she snapped open the folder in front of her. "Right, why don't we just start at the top of the list and go through the details point by point. You do have the list?" She glanced skeptically at the single manila folder in front of Antoine. It looked suspiciously flat.

He smiled at her. "It's all up here, my dear," he said, touching his forefinger to his temple. Then he winked.

Shelby stared at him for a second. "OK." She drew breath. "The schedule. Now, here's the way I have the timing worked out—"

"If I may interrupt." Antoine held up one hand and stopped Shelby dead. "If I may, my dear?" He gently took the schedule from Shelby, glanced at it, and put it aside. "May I be so bold as to make a few suggestions?"

Shelby opened her mouth to answer, but Antoine had directed the question toward Ann and Paul, who nodded.

"It is just a suggestion, of course. Never, never would I interfere," continued Antoine, looking scandalized at the very thought of doing such a thing. "But you must understand that I have worked here for ten years. You can trust me to take care of everything. Now I will tell you how best to organize the day and what has worked perfectly for many years here at this exact location where I have organized hundreds of weddings. And then you, bride and groom, you shall make your own decisions, of course. I just make suggestions." He paused.

"Antoine, we have a schedule." Shelby was not going down without a fight.

He looked at her kindly but sternly. Much the way you'd look at a puppy that had just made a mess on the rug. It wasn't her fault, but she had much to learn. He patted her on the shoulder. "You are in charge, my dear. You are completely in charge, of course." He threw his hands up in the air. "All I can do is make my little suggestions, if I may be allowed to do so. Suggestions based on my many years of experience." Here he glanced at the papers spread across the table. "I can see how hard you have been working. I have also been preparing." He opened the manila folder and removed the single sheet of paper it contained.

"Look, I have had this printed to put in a special place by the door so our guests will know exactly where to go." WEDDING GUESTS PLEASE PROCEED TO THE GRAND BALLROOM, said the sign. Shelby stared at the single sheet of paper that Antoine was holding and then looked pointedly at the reams of paper spread out across the table.

I caught Ann's eye, and we cracked up. She and Paul both had a good sense of humor, and it seemed we three had settled in to watch the fun.

"I have signs made already, thank you," Shelby said frostily.

"My dear, do you? Then we will certainly use your signs." Antoine looked outraged that anyone might suggest otherwise. "If you have signs, then why would we use any others? Everything I say is just a suggestion, my dear. Just, if I may, a little thought I am having to make things run as they should based on the fact that I have organized hundreds of weddings here that were all so lovely."

Antoine carefully slipped his sign back into the folder. There was a pause.

"I have a question," said Ann. "I was wondering about moving the ceremony to the other end of the ballroom. I think it might be prettier on that side, and then the guests could have cocktails in the lobby area while the room is set for dinner."

If she had been trying to break the tension, this was not the way to do it.

Shelby opened her mouth to respond, but Antoine got there first.

"Of course!" he was on his feet. "Exactly as it should be, my dear. That is how it is always done, and"—he paused to bow to Shelby—"with the greatest respect to my esteemed colleague, this is far, far better than the way you were previously planning."

Ann looked pleased. Shelby turned pink. She stood up, took a deep breath, dislodged a strand of hair from her lip gloss, and prepared to take back her hijacked wedding. "Ann, changing all our plans now is going to create a great deal of confusion. We have gone to a lot of trouble to arrange everything, and it is far too late in the day to start rearranging things now."

"Well, nooo, I don't think so," Antoine interrupted softly. He beamed at Ann. "You leave it all to me, my dear. I can rearrange things in the blink of an eye. No trouble at all." He snapped his fingers. "Like that, I have solved the problem. Five minutes' notice is all I ever need." He glanced at Shelby. "We professionals know how to do these things effortlessly, don't we, my dear? Now, here's how it will go."

From that point on, it was Antoine's show. He told us the entire schedule for the day, where to be and when, how the toasts and cake cutting would happen, and how much we would all enjoy ourselves. To Shelby's credit, she did try to interrupt a few times, but she was way out of her weight class. Antoine took Ann and Paul off to the other side of the ballroom to show them "exactly where we will perfectly arrange the chairs for your guests." Shelby looked stricken. I thought I'd see if I could make her feel a bit better. "Shelby, I had a couple of photography questions I wanted to check with you." But it was too late.

"Why don't you just go ask Antoine, then? He seems to have all the answers," she snapped.

"I am from Paris," Antoine was telling Ann and Paul when I joined them at the far side of the ballroom. "We French understand the art of celebration. Please know that your wedding is in my hands." Shelby had finished sorting out her papers and now joined us. She seemed somewhere between furious and on the verge of tears. Antoine took one look at Shelby and said, "Shelby and I are here to make everything perfect for you. We are a team seeing to your comfort." He turned to Shelby. "Please remember that I am also here to serve you, my dear. Whatever you need, you have only to ask." He made a small bow in her direction. She managed a frosty smile. Antoine, not in the least put off, smiled hugely in return.

"Now, Shelby, my dear, let us proceed to the hallway. I have a table to show you. A lovely table where you will arrange your little seating cards beautifully. And I can show you where the sign, yours or mine, can go to tell everyone the direction to take to this grand celebration. Come, all." Antoine linked his arm through Shelby's and headed for the door.

Ann, Paul, and I hung back for a moment.

"Do you think she'll kill him?" said Ann.

"No chance," said Paul. "He'll have her eating out of his hand by the wedding. It's a hearts-and-minds campaign. In any case, before she could try anything violent, he'd interrupt her with, if he may, just a little suggestion, but only a suggestion." We all cracked up.

Antoine looked back in our direction and waved happily.

I'd been having a great time, but there was probably some work waiting for me at home. There was always some work waiting for me at home. "Listen, you guys," I said, "it's been great, but I can't think of a single reason I need to be here, can you?"

Ann and Paul couldn't, so we shook hands all around and I told them I'd see them at the wedding. They headed off in the direction of the bar, where Antoine appeared to be buying Shelby a drink. Clearly, he was mending fences.

*T*he wedding went beautifully. Whenever I needed anything, Antoine was there. Shelby and her assistant bustled around a great deal and were never in sight when I actually needed something. They seemed to be spending most of their time back in a room they referred to as the staging area. Finally, when the party was going full throttle and I had a moment to catch my breath, I went to see what exactly was being staged in there. I found Shelby and her assistant sitting on the floor surrounded by petals that they were pulling off roses from the floral arrangements that had decorated the ceremony area. Shelby had rose petals in her hair. On a nearby table stood half a dozen glasses with the dregs of various colored cocktails in the bottom and a small mountain of damp-looking mini umbrellas, half-eaten pieces of sliced pineapple, and maraschino cherries. Just then a waiter arrived with two martini glasses filled with red liquid and decorated with orange and lime slices.

"Compliments of Mr. Antoine," he announced and put them on the table. He cleared away the remnants of the last four rounds and left.

"That Antoine," said Shelby, "he's a crazy guy. Did you see him sitting on the DJ's lap before? Those Frenchmen know how to throw a party! He's been sending us these things to try all night. He better stop soon or I won't be able to do my job." This cracked both of them up so much it took a while before they could explain what it was they were trying to do with the rose petals.

"We're going to take the shuttle bus over to the hotel and decorate the bedroom. The bride and groom's bedroom, I mean. Not ours." This started them laughing again.

With an effort, Shelby pulled herself together.

"It was my idea. Mine, not Antoine's. But he thinks it's great, and we think so, too." She looked confused for a minute. "I think so, too. Yes, so, we're just going to bag these glooms, I mean blooms, and then go decorate. Bottoms up." They both drained their glasses and got back to work pulling the petals off the roses.

Shelby looked happy.

As I left the room I bumped into Antoine.

"So," he said, "what do you think?"

"I think you've got everything under control," I said. "It's been a pleasure working with you."

"And you, too, of course, my dear." Antoine smiled happily. "Now, if I may make a suggestion? Just a suggestion, of course, you will do as you wish. But perhaps I could offer you a cocktail? I do so like to see all my fellow professionals happy."

30

All Shapes and Sizes

$\mathcal{S}$arah and I were having a discussion.

"There's no link between looks, money, and behavior," I said.

"That's crap and you know it." Sarah was looking glum.

"Nice language."

"If you're gonna hassle me about my language, I won't take the time to tell you how you should think about this."

"Sorry. OK, so tell me."

"Nice-looking brides are mean because they are spoiled. Brides who are challenged in the looks department act badly because they are bitter and disappointed people. Skinny brides are short-tempered because they are hungry. Hefty brides are angry because they feel rejected by society and bad about themselves. Wealthy brides are arrogant and impolite because they feel they are better than everyone else. Poor brides are snappy and sarcastic because they are exhausted from trying to figure out how to pay for everything." Sarah paused for breath. "None of them are any good."

"Sarah?"

"Don't ask."

Hmm. Sarah had shot a wedding by herself the night before. My guess was that it hadn't gone too well. She may not be not the world's cheeriest person, but she's not usually quite so cynical. I thought for a minute.

"What about Marianne? You can't have forgotten her?"

Sarah laughed. "Oh God, Marianne. I haven't thought about her in ages. They broke the mold when they made her. I don't know. Maybe you're right. Seems like most of the time the exceptions are the rule with your clients. Remember Marianne's dress?" I did—and everything else, too.

*M*arianne was certainly no beauty, but she was a peach. She was huge and happy and just couldn't help seeing the funny side of things. She and Steve were getting married in a small and slightly worn-down beach town. The ceremony was outdoors in a field overlooking the ocean, and the reception was at the local firehouse. Steve was a mellow, loose-limbed, unflappable sort of person. He was quick to smile and happiest driving his perfectly restored baby blue Mustang convertible along the coast road with the top down and stopping for a beer whenever he got the urge. He thought the sun rose and set over Marianne.

Marianne really had only one problem: She was just so darned happy all the time. It took a little while when you were with her to enter into her universe, but once you were there you got pretty happy yourself. Everything made Marianne laugh, and what a laugh it was. A great big Bette Midler belly laugh that shook all her chins and made the skin on her arms wobble.

When Sarah and I arrived at the little beach house she had rented to stay in the night before the wedding, we could hear her laugh as we came up the walkway. We squeezed into the tiny front room where Victor, the hairstylist, Marianne, and four of her friends were getting ready for the day and looked for a place to put down our bags. On the coffee table were several half-eaten sandwiches, a box of Krispy Kreme doughnuts, a large gray cat, and four champagne bottles crammed into an oversized ice bucket. It looked like Victor's makeup kit had exploded all over the room. One bridesmaid was painting her toenails while balancing on the arm of a very rickety couch. Another was bent double holding her bottom with one hand and a supersonic hairdryer in the other. This, it turned out, was the reason for Marianne's most recent burst of laughter. Victor had just opened a fresh bottle of champagne and the cork had bounced around the room, finally making painful contact with the backside of the bridesmaid who was drying her hair. All action now stopped while everyone toasted the lack of serious damage to the bridesmaid's bottom. Sarah gave me one of her "OK, we've landed in Crazy Town" looks. We squeezed ourselves into the space. Marianne climbed over the couch—the only way to get to us without trampling anyone—to give each of us a hug and a glass of champagne. Her hair was up in huge pink Velcro rollers, and she was wrapped in a bright yellow kimono.

"Champagne, Claire?"

"Maybe later. Let's keep these early shots in focus."

It wasn't that funny, but it was enough to send Marianne off into a fit of laughter that made champagne come out of her nose, which left all her bridesmaids hysterical. I looked at Sarah and Victor. Both of them were laughing like crazy, too. I've worked with Victor before. He's a perfectly nice guy, but to say he was fun to be around would be exaggerating wildly. Morose is more like it. But here he was offering to do the bridesmaids' hair for them while Marianne's curls set. For free! Stylists don't do that. Victor really doesn't do that. Then I heard Sarah saying she'd show the bridesmaids how to tie the sashes on their dresses. I decided to drink the champagne after all. This was too weird.

Marianne's cell phone rang. Steve had left his wedding shoes in San Francisco. He would have to wear sneakers or flip-flops. Marianne almost fell off her chair. "Yeah, baby, flips-flops. I love it. So chic." She laughed. "You'll look great." No wonder Steve was mellow. Victor took the curlers out of Marianne's hair.

"Oh, jeez." Marianne stared at herself in the mirror. Her smile faded. "I look like Shirley Temple." The room went quiet. She stood up, bent over, shook her head hard, and flipped back up. A huge wild mass of blond curls settled in disarray around her head.

"Voilà. Two hours' work to make me look exactly like I just rolled out of bed. I love it. Victor, you're a genius. A toast to Victor." We all toasted Victor. Several times.

Marianne's cell phone rang again. "He probably forgot his pants, too," hooted Marianne. "Well, looks like he'll be in his boxers and flip-flops." She answered the phone. "Hey, sweetie, what's up? Sure. Just come on over. Give me five minutes to get the old bod into the dress. Maybe ten, there's a lot of bod." She snapped shut the phone. "Come on, ladies, grab your shoehorns and roll up your sleeves. It's time to get me into that dress. Steve wants to stop by and say hello. I think he misses me."

$\mathcal{G}$etting Marianne into that dress was no simple matter. If Marianne herself was large, her dress was the size of a tent. She had designed it herself, and the skirt was a huge billowing cream puff made up of multiple layers of white satin and tulle. The dangerously low-cut bustier top was encrusted with crystal beads. Marianne was not afraid of cleavage. That bustier alone took two people on each side squeezing the back together while Sarah frantically tried to hook the hooks. I looked for flattering angles and tried not to step on anybody while I took pictures. We all worked up quite a sweat. Victor sat on the couch shouting unhelpful directions until we threatened to make him help us with the bustier. That shut him up. Marianne laughed through it all and kept telling us to "put some elbow grease into it." We stopped a lot for champagne breaks. When we finally had all of Marianne inside her dress, hooked, zippered, and buttoned up, we stood back to catch our breath and take a look. She was magnificent. Jewel-encrusted, sexy, and positively stately.

"Make way for the queen," she said and headed for the door. It was a small doorway. I remembered the Winnie-the-Pooh story I had read to my daughter when she was younger. The one where Pooh eats too much honey while visiting Rabbit and gets lodged in Rabbit's doorway. He ends up stuck there until he loses weight. I began to worry about getting Marianne to her ceremony and caught Sarah's eye. We moved in behind Marianne. Just as she hit the doorway we both gave her a good shove. She popped right through.

"Whoa there, guys," yelped Marianne. "What's the hurry?"

We apologized. "Just trying to make sure we're right behind you and don't miss any great shots," I panted.

Marianne looked at me. "Sure you weren't trying to be certain my big ol' self got through that tiny little doorway?"

I started to deny it, then realized that she knew exactly what we were up to and, as usual, thought it was hilarious. "Wait till I tell Steve how you two had to shove me through. That's what I call dedication to your work. Hey, did anyone bring out any of that champagne?" She picked up the massive bunch of pink peonies that the florist had left for her. She looked like nothing so much as an enormous white peony herself.

When Steve and Marianne came to pick up their wedding pictures after a three-week honeymoon in Bermuda, Marianne was a mess. She was wearing a tank top as though to advertise the fact that her entire right arm, from shoulder to wrist, was a giant scab. It wasn't pretty. Neither was her face. A huge scrape, partially scabbed over and raw looking, covered most of her right cheek.

"Mopeds," hooted Marianne when she saw my expression. "Those little suckers scoot right out from under you."

Steve laughed. "We rented a couple of those crazy mopeds, and Marianne kept trying to do stunts."

"Well, you know what, Steve," said Marianne, "I figure, if you love me when I look like this, then you'll love me no matter what." And she laughed.

Sarah and I had been talking about Marianne for a while. Marianne led to Tina and her shady uncle who kept trying to figure out ways to pay me as a business expense, then changed his mind and arrived unannounced on my doorstep with three thousand dollars in cash (presumably in unmarked bills), and then changed his mind again and asked for his cash back and wrote me a personal check. Tina's uncle reminded Sarah about Colleen, who discovered on her wedding day that her dress didn't fit properly, threw a fit, and then decided it was perfect if she wore it backward. Then we had to discuss poor Janet, whose future father-in-law died just weeks before the wedding; the groom's mother insisted that the wedding go on anyway but everyone had to wear dark colors and be appropriately somber. Janet walked down the aisle to funeral music. That led to memories of the disastrous wedding where the flower girl went exploring in the bushes and got bitten by a rattlesnake. "Puts quite a damper on the day when your flower girl gets airlifted out by helicopter," said Sarah. She looked a lot happier. (In case you're wondering, the flower girl was fine. Even Sarah in a bad mood doesn't think deadly accidents are funny.)

"Quite a bunch, your clients," said Sarah. "I have to admit, we've had a lot of crazy ones, but some have been pretty darn great. No shortage of laughs, either."

"Want to tell me about last night now?" I asked.

"Last night? Oh, forget it. Just give me a couple of days and we'll turn it into a story. Hey, remember that tuxedo-wearing bulldog that fainted at the beach?"

31

War Zone Work

$\mathcal{O}$nce upon a time I saw myself in refugee camps and prisons. I imagined that I would use my camera to tell important stories and expose great injustices. Don't get me wrong, I'm not mourning the lost dreams of my youth. I'm not at all sure I won't still end up in some pretty interesting places. Generally I like what I do. Once in a while I love it. It is difficult, various, creative, demanding, hardly ever boring, and often hilariously funny. It is also annoying, depressing, and stressful. It makes my feet hurt and leaves me questioning the nature of love and human relationships. What more could you ask for?

Like any other profession, the world of wedding photography is filled with a wide variety of types. There are hacks and jerks, and there are very talented and perceptive people. Though the wedding photographer's reputation is not quite as bad as it used to be, the guy in the bad suit who insists on the nightmare photo shoot that lasts two hours while his assistant-wife organizes everyone by height is still out there. Part of the problem is the fact that the stereotypes make for the best stories. The photographers who arrive with ridiculous props, shoot in soft focus, and digitally insert a full moon or a sunset are the ones everyone tells tales about. They will happily superimpose the faces of the bride and groom over a champagne glass, suggest "natural" poses, and carefully stage a thousand spontaneous moments. You can go online and find plenty of wedding photography Web sites with references to capturing precious moments, priceless memories, and the timeless beauty of your special day. The photographers' bios will tell you they love weddings and every moment of what they do. Perhaps they do.

Personally, I don't have a strong affinity for weddings. I have sometimes been moved by the obvious affection between a bride and groom, but I don't love weddings in general. What interests me is the drama—to be present, to witness, and to document the intense strain and joy of this kind of gathering. Everything happens at weddings. It is by no means all sweetness and celebration. There is anger, jealousy, sadness. Quirks of character are heightened. Old arguments are patched up or made newly sensitive. People remember their own weddings, the loss of youth and love. They think of time wasted or well spent. There are revelations of great vanity and self-obsession, and other times when a couple seem to lose themselves entirely in each other and the moment. With wedding photography there is also the satisfaction of creating something that will give pleasure and tell the truth at the same time, of doing something that is important to those involved, of creating a visual memory. Sometimes the people I am dealing with are spoiled or selfish or completely unaware of their good fortune. There are moments, though, when I get a glimpse of the grace and the hopefulness of it all, and that is wonderful.

Occasionally, perhaps when I'm listening to yet another cover band mangle "Brown-Eyed Girl," I wonder how I got here. When I've nearly been run over by a conga line, or I'm being propositioned yet again by the bride's drunken uncle, I think that none of this is anything I could have imagined myself doing. But here I am. I look around, have a glass of champagne, photograph some crazy moment between two of the guests, and remember how much I enjoy the art and unpredictability of what I do. So I try to do my work well. I relish my freedom and take the best photographs I can. I'll never know if a war zone would have made me happier, but I can make a pretty good guess. Besides, if I'm feeling reckless, there are plenty of risks right here in wedding land.